'*Unleashing Great Teaching* is a remarkable book. It combines research on adult learning and the authors' hands-on experiences of working with schools to produce an accessible, practical, and at times entertaining "how to" for improving teacher learning. Should be on the desk of every school leader in the country (if not the world).'

Lucy Crehan, *teacher, education explorer and international education consultant, UK*

Unleashing Great Teaching

It's within the power of each and every school to unleash the best in teachers, day by day, month by month, year by year.

This practical handbook takes the guesswork out of professional learning, showing school leaders how they can build a self-improving culture and remove barriers to learning. David Weston and Bridget Clay set out their advice for how every school can bring in the best ideas from the whole system, and make sure that these have a lasting effect in the classroom. Packed full of examples, easy-to-use ideas and checklists, *Unleashing Great Teaching* brings together a vast body of experience gained by the Teacher Development Trust (UK), and shows how other schools can learn from these insights. From fostering a culture of evaluating impact to establishing good relationships, communication and a developmental culture, this book takes each and every aspect of the school system and reassesses its role as a driver of teacher and student success.

An invaluable resource for leaders at any level within the schooling system, *Unleashing Great Teaching* will open doors and inspire leaders, teachers, students and communities to learn about learning.

David Weston is the Founder and Chief Executive of the Teacher Development Trust. In March 2015, he was appointed by the Department for Education as Chair of the Teachers' Professional Development Expert Group.

Bridget Clay is currently Head of Programme for Leading Together at Teach First, and was previously Director of School Programmes at the Teacher Development Trust, the national charity for professional learning in the UK.

Unleashing Great Teaching

The Secrets to the Most Effective
Teacher Development

David Weston and Bridget Clay

Routledge
Taylor & Francis Group

LONDON AND NEW YORK

First published 2018
by Routledge
2 Park Square, Milton Park, Abingdon, Oxon OX14 4RN

and by Routledge
711 Third Avenue, New York, NY 10017

Routledge is an imprint of the Taylor & Francis Group, an informa business

British Library Cataloguing-in-Publication Data
A catalogue record for this book is available from the British Library

Library of Congress Cataloguing-in-Publication Data
Names: Weston, David, 1979- author. | Clay, Bridget, author.
Title: Unleashing great teaching: the secrets to the most effective teacher development / David Weston and Bridget Clay.
Description: Abingdon, Oxon; New York, NY: Routledge, 2018. | Includes bibliographical references.
Identifiers: LCCN 2018000329 (print) | LCCN 2018014617 (ebook) | ISBN 9781315101729 (eb) | ISBN 9781138105935 (hbk) | ISBN 9781138105997 (pbk) | ISBN 9781315101729 (ebk)
Subjects: LCSH: Effective teaching. | Teachers–Training of.
Classification: LCC LB1025.3 (ebook) | LCC LB1025.3 .W42 2018 (print) | DDC 371.102–dc23
LC record available at https://lccn.loc.gov/2018000329

ISBN: 978-1-138-10593-5 (hbk)
ISBN: 978-1-138-10599-7 (pbk)
ISBN: 978-1-315-10172-9 (ebk)

Typeset in Minion Pro
by Deanta Global Publishing Services, Chennai, India

Printed and bound in Great Britain by
TJ International Ltd, Padstow, Cornwall

Contents

Acknowledgements

This book has been a labour of many hours of discussion, reading, writing and editing. It's impossible to thank everyone who has inspired us along the way, but we do have to offer some particular thanks.

First, thank you to our partners and families for putting up with us disappearing with laptops, morning, noon and night, in leisure time, on holiday and when we really should have known better. Thank you for reading our work, being patient and knowing just the right time to ask, 'shouldn't you be writing right now?'

Thank you to the team at Routledge for taking on this project and for your patience and understanding as deadlines whistled by!

Thank you to our colleagues at the Teacher Development Trust and everyone who fed back on early drafts.

Thank you to the amazing researchers and bloggers who have inspired us. To Philippa Cordingley, Rob Coe, Steve Higgins, Toby Greany and all the authors of the *Developing Great Teaching* report which underpinned so much of this book.

Finally, thank you to all the schools and teachers we have worked with, who have shared, discussed and unpicked their practice. You endlessly shape our thinking and are ultimately the reason that this book exists.

About the authors

David Weston is the Founder and Chief Executive of the Teacher Development Trust, the UK's national charity for effective professional development in schools and colleges.

In March 2015 he was appointed by the Department for Education as Chair of the Teachers' Professional Development Expert Group. He was a founding Director of the Chartered College of Teaching. David has written and spoken extensively in the media about teaching and teacher development and has had a number of radio and TV appearances discussing both teaching and LGBT issues, including a TEDx talk in the USA. He tweets as @informed_edu and has over 26,000 followers.

Bridget Clay is a former teacher who works supporting schools to implement powerful professional learning. She is the Head of Programme for Leading Together at Teach First, a UK-based charity focused on ending educational inequality. Previously, she was the Director of School Programmes at the Teacher Development Trust, the national charity for professional learning in the UK.

She has advised and supports a number of organisations, including the Department for Education and the Greater London Authority. As a speaker, she frequently appears at conferences and events, including ResearchED and The Telegraph Festival of Education. She is a regular media contributor, including for TES, SecEd and Headteacher Update, and has contributed to a book for National Education Trust, edited by Marc Rowland.

Foreword

By Dame Alison Peacock

This handbook is for leaders of professional learning, leaders of teams and for all those interested in developing their own practice as evaluative practitioners. Throughout the book, we are constantly reminded of the vital importance of linking professional learning to the difference we seek to make in the classroom for the benefit of students. The reader is engaged and entertained with stories of practice drawn from the authors' experience of working with primary and secondary schools across England. These illustrative examples bring to life the key messages of the book. Alongside useful references for further reading there are helpful summaries of terminology, and throughout there is recognition of new insights gained through cognitive learning science.

Why does professional learning matter so much?

The notion of the journey of novice towards expert illustrates the need for teachers to continually seek opportunities to build pedagogical knowledge combined with subject expertise. A core message is that the best professional learning is contextualised and rooted in both theory and practice. Examples are given of ways to rigorously link every initiative to shared goals that explicitly lead to student success. We see the power of teacher agency where the desired outcomes both for the individual teacher and the school community align thereby achieving optimal impact.

Leadership

Leadership of professional learning within a culture of opportunity and trust is celebrated. Within this, the importance of leaders modelling their own ongoing development journey is emphasised. A link is made between wellbeing of colleagues and the reduction of stress or threat that comes with high levels of agency. The key role of governance and leadership of learning for everyone within the school community is shown. Governance that recognises the need to allocate resource for professional learning is clearly seen to be important within the wider context of school development and student outcomes.

Getting the culture right

Building a culture where professional learning is at the heart is shown to be highly effective. Colleagues within schools or groups of schools where professional learning is embedded and is responsive are likely to flourish, thereby enabling their students to thrive. A culture of dialogic exchange about pedagogy within the context of coaching conversations is presented as a model of continuous learning. However, the importance of external expertise is also recognised. Within such a culture there is a positive opportunity to use performance management as a resource for review and growth.

Practical steps

Alongside a clear rationale for principled leadership that enables teachers' careers to flourish are detailed practical actions to support this process. Useful advice for preparation and delivery of presentations is included with reference to issues such as the risk of cognitive overload. Techniques such as the use of video clips, models of timetabling, checklists for coaching conversations and suggestions for innovations such as journal clubs and staff access to research are explained. An approach to rigorous lesson study that focuses on students and encourages pedagogical dialogue, with reference to evidence, is described. All of this within a recommended annual professional learning plan.

Impact at scale

The issues explored within this book focus on the vital importance of building a teaching profession that is increasingly skilled and informed by the emerging evidence base about teaching and learning. It is within this context that the new Chartered College of Teaching begins to grow membership and to offer the potential for enhanced professional status. At a time when school-based initial teacher training is prevalent in England and when there is an imperative to provide career pathways that attract and retain our teachers, this book addresses an urgent need to establish a culture of high-quality professional learning for all. I urge you to engage practically with this text. For too long, our energies have focused too much on judging teachers instead of building a culture where they are intellectually stimulated and supported in their desire to build and refine expertise.

Introduction

What if we were to put as much effort into developing teachers as we did into developing students? How do we find a way to put the collective expertise of our profession at every teacher's fingertips? Why can't we make every school a place where teachers thrive and students succeed?

Well, we can. And in this book, we're going to show you how. We believe that it is within every teacher to be better next year than they are this year. It is within the power of every school and school system to unleash teachers' best, day by day, month by month and year by year.

We had two different teaching career paths but have ended up sharing a deep-seated drive to right a wrong at the heart of the school system – how we support and grow teachers. Writing together has forced us to go back to the drawing board and re-evaluate this passion. It has forced us to critically examine things we thought we knew and things we were unconsciously avoiding.

As former teachers, we both have our own experiences of professional learning and support in school. While teaching we both frequently fell into the trap of over-enthusiasm, where new ideas were tried out immediately but often discarded and forgotten within a week or two. But we also developed a real dissatisfaction with the superficial advice and support that teachers often receive.

Every lesson is a precious resource. Every teacher wants to squeeze out every drop of value, but somehow schools are not always well set up to support this.

Hopefully, all teachers have experienced that magic feeling of seeing something that they have learnt change things for the better for their students. Sadly, many teachers also experience frustrations, struggling to keep on top of the challenges and changes that are needed.

We got into teaching because we are fascinated and delighted by learning; watching light bulbs start glowing as children learn, or watching the sense of accomplishment and joy when a struggle turns into a secure skill. We have taken that love into our work with teachers and it's no less satisfying.

We have seen that professional learning is key to supporting teachers. It helps their morale, their efficacy and their motivation. We've sat in rooms with teachers who've wept tears of frustration and with teachers who are bursting with renewed excitement.

Getting learning right for the adults in our schools is crucial to retaining and recruiting a vibrant and successful workforce. But professional learning is not just important for staff; it is the means through which we help teachers to support and teach their students, and is imperative for enabling them to realise the potential of the students we teach.

Three big ideas

Jane was an experienced teacher of fifteen years. She was head of the Geography department and, according to the school Principal, 'an absolute stalwart, totally reliable and brilliant'. We stepped in to interview her as part of our research into the school. The Principal beamed at the three of us as she closed the door behind us.

Jane looked at us warily as we sat down. 'Thank you for meeting us. We can reassure you that this is all completely confidential.' She visibly relaxed.

'We're here to find out what it's like to be a teacher at this school. Please could you tell us about your own professional learning here? How have you been growing and developing? What's it like to work here?'

Jane looked at us, took a breath, and sighed.

'I feel completely trapped. I'm "reliable Jane", sent in to fix colleagues or tell them what to do. I really care about the students here and I know that our school is in a mess. But I didn't get into the job for this.'

'Everything here is about paperwork: measuring, monitoring. Everything is about consistency and looking good in inspections. I can't tell you how many sessions I've been asked to deliver on "being outstanding". I spend my evenings working on spreadsheets for my department to send chunks of data to senior leaders, to give them something to write in reports.'

'You asked me to talk about my learning. You know what? Nobody has given me any development opportunities since I can remember. It's all about telling others, fixing problems or hiding them. I was doing a Master's dissertation in my last school. But that's all gone now.'

'I don't know how much longer I can do this.'

★★★

We would like to say that this was a one-off, but sadly this sort of story is all too common here in England. Yet, we've spoken to teachers who are bursting with enthusiasm and seen classrooms which are steeped in learning.

What's the secret? In this book we focus on three big ideas which lie at the heart of the solution.

Focusing on the *organisational edge*

Imagine a school as a circle. All of the staff, leaders, policies, procedures and systems lie within the centre of the circle and, at the edge, staff and systems interact with students, families and communities. This edge is the important line, where impact is created through the interaction with the complex and dynamic outside world. The centre of the circle – all of the leadership, the systems and resources – ideally supports the organisation to be effective at its edge.

The edge is where teachers work in classrooms. It's where conversations take place with parents, interactions between adults and students in corridors and on playing fields.

Schools are incredibly complicated places. No two students are the same, no two parents are the same and every member of staff brings their own unique personality. The complexities are ever-changing; as anyone who has worked in a school will know, everything can change rapidly. The organisational edge is therefore where the organisation must respond to the greatest complexity and change. It is where the impact is really happening, where the nimblest responses to the messy complexity are enacted.

Sadly, too many schools turn their focus away. The organisation becomes inward-looking, focused on rules, compliance and bureaucracy. Professional learning becomes about consistency, not excellence.

This book is a manifesto for focusing back on the edge. We explain what needs to be happening in the centre of the organisation to deliver powerful learning for students, families and communities that they work with.

Empowering *evaluative practitioners* to engage in *Responsive Professional Learning*

Evaluative practitioners are teachers and staff who constantly assess the impact of their practice and professional learning on students. In a school that is driven by success at the organisational edge, all teachers and staff need to have the ability and support to best direct their own practice and their own learning and development of that practice to what is happening at the edge.

In many schools, leaders claim to be the ones doing the measuring, evaluating and checking. Teachers are given the job of delivery – delivering teaching to children and assessment data scores to senior leaders. But it is the leaders who feel they must make the interpretations and pass judgement on what must happen next. This is toxic. It squashes any curiosity and ingenuity in the school's most valuable asset: its staff. It slows down reactions to issues, it prioritises the generic over the detailed and it takes away any sense of agency from teachers.

Responsive Professional Learning is where all the programmes, activities and principles of new learning for staff are driven by and respond to what is happening at the organisational edge. Responsive Professional Learning enables success at the organisational edge and enables teachers and staff to become evaluative practitioners.

Unresponsive development is about broadcasting ideas at teachers. It is about sharing fads and fashions, irrespective of relevance and context. We've seen too many experienced teachers for whom the words 'professional development' become code for boredom and disrespect.

But schools can do better. We'll explain how to make teachers into evaluative practitioners, able to engage in ongoing improvement and learning that is responsive to their students' needs. By harnessing the ingenuity of every person in the building, schools can become truly great.

Drawing on collective expertise

There is already far more research on effective teaching than any one teacher could learn in a lifetime. Students deserve better than simply being lucky if their teacher knows the best way to meet their needs. Teachers deserve better than having to guess how to do the best for their students.

From now on, every teacher needs to be able to draw upon the collective expertise of the whole profession, not just the ideas already in their head, not just the best ideas in their school. This is a simple, yet powerful idea. Every teacher in every school needs to be linked into national networks of knowledge. Every professional learning opportunity needs to tap into the best ideas out there, not just an idea that feels new or interesting within their school.

This idea opens new avenues for teachers to become experts in more specialist areas and to use this expertise to have impact on more students. It allows us to recognise and develop great knowledge and skill, breaking the increasingly illogical link between management seniority and supposed expertise in teaching.

Why this book?

Through our work at the Teacher Development Trust, working with hundreds of schools in England, Wales and beyond, we have seen many different contexts and different approaches to professional learning and how they have been successful. This book is designed as a handbook for leaders of professional learning, leaders of teams and anyone in a school interested in developing their practice.

It draws on our work with schools, school leaders, researchers and policy makers. It draws on evidence from education, psychology, leadership and broader organisational effectiveness. While any one chapter here could be a whole book in itself, we hope that this book can open doors and start great journeys of learning about learning. We also include plenty of practical ideas that can be implemented straight away.

What do we mean by 'professional learning'?

In this book, we take a broad definition of professional learning: any process aimed at changing awareness, thinking or the practice of adults working in schools. However, within that, it is useful to separate out the different purposes of professional learning. We distinguish between professional learning that is directly targeted at benefitting students' learning (such as learning focused on improving students' literacy or their understanding of geometry) from professional learning that might more indirectly link to classroom practice and student learning (such as learning focused on health and safety, leadership or structuring a timetable). This is something we explore further in Chapter Three, 'Impact: implementing and evaluating professional learning'.

We examine a great variety of different activities and processes. 'Professional learning' is often assumed to be external input, a course or a speaker, or a discreet programme. Other writers often try and distinguish between 'learning new information' and 'turning that learning into new practice and activities that benefit students'. In this book, the term *professional learning* encompasses all those activities. Meeting time, informal conversations, peer observations and experimentation in the classroom should all be recognised as facets of professional learning. We also distinguish between individual professional learning activities versus professional learning programmes which thread multiple activities and opportunities together.

Terminology

The arena of professional learning has turned into a terminology and acronym soup. Common terms include:

- Professional Development (PD)
- Professional Learning (PL)
- Continuing (or occasionally Continuous) Professional Development (CPD)
- Joint Practice Development (JPD)
- Continuing Professional Development and Learning (CPDL)
- Continuing Professional Learning and Development (CPLD)

- Professional Learning Communities (PLCs)
- In-service Training (INSET)

While a few people try to sharply distinguish between the meanings of these terms, we rarely find such clarity in schools. More often than not, people take a new term and apply it to existing practices.

Our approach is to keep it simple. We feel that it is unhelpful to try and separate learning and development, so the terms are reasonably interchangeable. The addition of 'continuing' or 'continuous' seems to have made little difference in practice so we tend to remove it, for simplicity, while acknowledging that the acronym *CPD* is probably the most widely used in the United Kingdom, while *PD* is most widely used elsewhere.

This will, inevitably, irritate the very small minority who have managed to sharply define terms in their heads, but we shall cautiously risk their ire in the pursuit of simplicity.

We also use the term *students* throughout this book. This is certainly the standard international term, but we acknowledge that there are teachers in the United Kingdom who feel the term is only appropriate in secondary and tertiary education, not primary. We ask for forgiveness from primary colleagues here in the United Kingdom and hope that you can accept that this book is just as rooted in the primary phase of education as it is in the secondary.

We also often refer to *teachers* as a short-hand for *educators and staff that work with students*. A school is a community of staff that work together for the best for students. In the best schools, all staff members work as a coherent team, with every adult carefully supported to play their part in education. It is a foolish (and usually ineffective) school leader that puts up artificial barriers between teachers and other staff.

While many of the ideas here are applicable for all staff, we try to identify lessons for specific groups of staff at certain points. In particular, we occasionally highlight ideas for teaching assistants, sometimes known as learning support assistants or classroom aides.

Finally, much of this book has been inspired by the schools we have worked with and which have been generous enough to share their practice. Yet, all schools described in the book are a product of this inspiration, rather than specific named examples, and any school names used are made up.

The ingredients of effective professional learning

Unfortunately, there is no easy checklist for effective professional learning. However, there are a few key ingredients. We explore all of these in greater depth later in the book.

Focus – what are teachers working on?

For professional learning to benefit students, participants need to maintain a clear focus on student learning and outcomes. It is easy to slip into a list of what teachers should be doing rather than which students will benefit and how. The big question should be: 'has my learning made a difference yet?' This helps prompt the questions 'what difference am I trying to make?' and 'how will I know if I've made a difference?'.

- Teachers should be involved in identifying the student needs in their classroom. This means being clear on what is being learnt and how it fits the bigger picture. It means being clear on the habits, behaviours and attitudes of successful students.

- There needs to be engagement with the theory of what might help. This means understanding how students learn: how knowledge, skill and capability are developed. It means engaging critically with research, identifying which approaches and practices are likely to maximise precious classroom time so that students succeed.
- Teachers need to be involved in putting ideas into practice. This means conducting carefully supported experiments with approaches that are new to them. It requires seeing approaches modelled by experts and implementing and adapting those for their own classroom, as well as regular practice and quality feedback.
- Teachers need to evaluate the impact of these practices on those students in the classroom. This means checking whether a practice is working for the students and improving outcomes. These outcomes could include attainment, attitudes or behaviours – certainly this definition goes far beyond standardised tests and school accountability measures. By focusing their own learning on improving outcomes, teachers become *evaluative practitioners* who are engaging in *Responsive Professional Learning*.
- Finally, professional learning should also take into account teachers' prior knowledge and thinking. One size rarely fits all. For any given practice there will be teachers for whom it is new and teachers for whom it appears old-hat. Some will react warmly towards it, some will want to reject it. Some will find it helpful, others patronising. The best professional learning takes this into account.

Timing and structure of professional learning

Habits can be hard to change. It takes a long time to change things we do day-in and day-out. Teachers need time, space, high-quality expertise and facilitation in an atmosphere of trust and respect.

Only specific bits of new information can be effectively learnt in a one-off session. To change everyday practice that impacts on students, professional learning needs to be sustained over time. In addition, there should be multiple opportunities for teachers to engage in new learning, experiment with their practice and evaluate its impact on students.

We explore the idea of regular, repeated opportunities to structure professional learning. This creates a *rhythm* of professional learning, beating like a heart through teaching practice instead of being an unwelcome add-on, tacked on awkwardly to the end of terms or semesters. It allows professional learning to repeat and refine practices with increasing depth – i.e. *iterative* development.[1]

Many schools now offer weekly or fortnightly professional learning time which is focused on ongoing collaboration, planning and assessment. Well-designed collaboration is a key part of effective professional learning. In effective schools, whole staff briefings are minimised, subject and team meetings are kept as free of briefing and administrative work as possible, and the focus is on improving and sharing teaching knowledge and practice in direct response to student needs.

Engaging with external expertise

When engaging in a professional learning process, teachers want to be sure that they are getting good advice. This means ensuring that professional learning is informed by a strong evidence base.

This might be enabled through engaging directly with research journals; some schools are creating specific 'Research Lead' roles within schools to facilitate this. Professional learning is most effective when it includes both engagement with theory and practical experimentation in the classroom. An effective professional learning programme must include both.

However, this is an area with endless pitfalls. Simply asking 'what works best?' and doing exactly that is no guarantee of success. For example, the Education Endowment Foundation suggest that helping teachers to give better feedback should be our number one priority.[2] However, Kluger and DeNisi found that 38% of feedback interventions actually had a negative impact on student outcomes.[3] Engaging with expertise is not straightforward, and we suggest some strategies to support this.

External expertise has a much greater role than just choosing what to try. We are all awash with psychological biases and narrow perspectives that resist change. Our minds work surprisingly hard to protect our existing thinking or sneakily return to old thought-patterns. Great professional learning requires expert facilitators *to make it a disruptive process* that helps us overcome the limitations of our own thinking.

Effective professional learning connects staff to good practice and thinking, perhaps through subject and specialist association memberships, research bulletins, conferences and social media. However, it should also be recognised that to embed this knowledge it is necessary to work with external experts and facilitators who can support, challenge, model practice and inspire colleagues (Figure 0.1).

Culture

Culture is one of the more elusive, but also more important aspects that enables an effective professional learning process or programme within a school. It can be hard to pin down what makes an effective culture, yet nearly everyone can easily compare a more positive or negative one. Kraft and Papay explored this area and found that where teachers reported low levels of support, development and trust, performance of these teachers seemed to plateau after just a few years.[4] However, where teachers reported much higher levels of support, they not only improved faster in their early career, they kept on improving year after year. Where the culture is right, teachers will develop to better meet their students' needs.

Saying a **conference** is "great professional development" ... is like saying that a **shopping** trip is a "good meal"

It's what you **do** with what you **bring back** that counts

FIGURE 0.1   Theory into practice.

So what are the possible areas that impact on culture?

- **Vision for professional learning** – The importance of professional learning should be widely understood and discussed. It is there not to tick accountability boxes but to help students succeed. In the best schools, everyone sees professional learning as a top priority. This is reinforced where leaders are able to model their own professional learning and take part in professional learning processes.
- **Time and resources available** – time and money are always in short supply. Yet if professional learning is not something that is prioritised with time and money, it probably won't be seen as a priority by anyone else.
- **Observing and evaluating teachers** – lesson observations can be a very effective part of a professional learning process. However, if observations come with high-stake consequences or unhelpful feedback, they fail to support teachers and good practice and instead encourage jumping through hoops.
- **Performance management** – clunky appraisal systems that rely only on annual, formulaic conversations are unlikely to develop day to day practice. Worse still, if also combined with high-stake assessments of teachers they result in stress and pressure, rather than challenge or support. Many schools are moving towards more frequent and more formative appraisal systems.
- **Permission to fail** – For someone to change their practice, they must learn and be prepared to try something new, which may or may not work. Schools that recognise, encourage and celebrate this are much more likely to build a developmental culture.
- **Communication** – At the heart of professional learning is great communication. This develops shared understanding, trust and effective challenge. Good-quality dialogue allows teams to look at difficult issues and stops problems from becoming major barriers.
- **Leadership and management** – the culture of professional learning is set from the top. Inclusive, inspiring leadership produces a very different culture from autocratic, controlling approaches. Good leaders encourage teachers, just as good teachers encourage their students, to keep improving and pushing for greater success. It is this that will lead to a genuine process of continuing professional development.

We describe some of the ways and approaches that schools have adopted this culture in Chapter Four.

Notes

1   Cordingley, P., Higgins, S., Greany, T., Buckler, N., Coles-Jordan, D., Crisp, B., Saunders, L., & Coe, R. (2015). Developing great teaching: Lessons from the international reviews into effective professional development. *Teacher Development Trust*. http://TDTrust.org/about/dgt

2   Higgins, S., Katsipataki, M., Kokotsaki, D., Coleman, R., Major, L.E., & Coe, R. (2014). *The Sutton Trust-Education Endowment Foundation Teaching and Learning Toolkit*. London: Education Endowment Foundation.

3   Kluger, A. N., & DeNisi, A. (1996). The effects of feedback interventions on performance: A historical review, a meta-analysis, and a preliminary feedback intervention theory. *Psychological Bulletin, 119*(2), 254–284.

4   Kraft, M.A., & Papay, J.P. (2014). Can professional environments in schools promote teacher development? Explaining heterogeneity in returns to teaching experience. *Educational Evaluation and Policy Analysis*. https://scholar.harvard.edu/mkraft/publications/can-professional-environments-schools-promote-teacher-development-explaining

one
Teacher
learning
The building blocks

Phil will never forget his first driving lesson. His instructor, Len, was a reassuring figure: calm, soft-spoken and never in a rush. Len's car was an old Renault with super soft suspension and a faint smell of lemon air freshener.

Stepping through the driver's door into that seat was an odd experience. Everything felt familiar after the seventeen years Phil had spent as a passenger, and yet everything was also very new. First there was the physical closeness of all the controls, the three pedals, the wheel and gear stick. But then there was the sensation of just looking at the road from a new perspective, clutching the keys in his hand with a sense of anticipation.

Phil remembers Len looking at him and smiling: 'We won't go far unless you put the key in the ignition, you know.' Okay, so this was actually happening!

Len asked Phil to push the accelerator slightly to get a feel for it, then to press the clutch and move into first gear. He explained biting point, asking Phil to gently release the clutch and gently press the accelerator. Obviously, Phil immediately stalled.

Len chuckled and told him not to worry. On the second go he managed it, and then released the hand brake. Excitement and horror – they were moving!

Suddenly, instructions were coming faster. Look in the rear mirror, look in the side mirror, use the indicator, move your foot to the brake, change gear, look over your shoulder, keep both hands on the steering wheel, be aware of that car. Everything started happening at once. Everything was unfamiliar. Phil felt overwhelmed with all the jobs and forgot the clutch. They stalled.

Thump.

'Don't worry,' said Len, 'you'll get familiar. Let's try again.'

***

Phil's first driving lesson is a great reminder of what a new teacher is going through. Every teacher has spent many years in a classroom before they begin the job, but never as the person in charge. Things are both familiar and unfamiliar. Everyone brings baggage from their schooldays, but also must come to terms with being in charge of thirty children or young adults, smoothly directing the lesson, watching the timing, giving feedback, constantly scanning the room, maintaining self-awareness, operating electronic systems, locating and distributing books, and so many other things.

The fact that we can be both experienced and inexperienced at the same time is just one of the reasons that teacher learning is a complex process.

A model of learning and remembering

What's actually going on when you learn something new? Sweller (1988)[1] suggested that learning is a process of changing what's stored in your *long-term memory*. It involves gradually moving along a scale from *novice* to *expert*.

Let's use a very simplified model of the learning process, based on the work of Atkinson and Shiffrin (1968)[2] and Baddeley and Hitch (1974)[3] (see Figure 1.1).

In this model we've got a few key elements.

Sensory memory is a super short-term memory. It maintains an impression of everything you have just heard, seen, tasted, smelled or felt.

Attention is the process of focusing on certain sensations that are in the sensory memory. If you think about the little finger on your right hand then you will be aware of what it is touching, how warm it is, whether it feels uncomfortable or not.

Up until you thought about it, you probably hadn't been aware of those sensations. But it is possible to deliberately direct your attention, thereby ignoring other sensations.

Attention is not always deliberately directed. If you step on a sharp stone, then you suddenly become aware of your feet. If you are working on a piece of writing, then you can sometimes become distracted by perceived hunger, thirst, tiredness, threat, etc. – i.e. the sorts of things that we've evolved to pay attention to in order to help us survive.

In that first driving lesson, *Len* was helping direct attention to the most relevant and important sensations around him.

In the development of teaching, we want to help teachers stay focused on the most relevant sensations and information to avoid confusion and distraction.

Working memory is where we temporarily store sensations or ideas – it's like a temporary jotting pad. It has very limited capacity; we can only store a few elements at once. However, there are thought to be two distinct channels within working memory: the first is sounds and words, the second is images and shapes. The two channels work in parallel. We can learn more when the information coming into both channels is complementary. We refer to this in Chapter Six when exploring effective delivery of expertise.

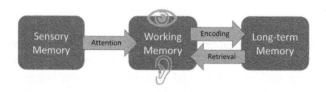

FIGURE 1.1   A simplified model of memory and learning.

Even though working memory is very limited, we often 'cheat' the limits by remembering a block of information as a single chunk. E.g. the word 'moon' doesn't require four spaces, one for each letter, M – O – O – N, as we are able to quickly match the pattern of the word to our long-term memory of the word 'moon' and just keep the memory of the whole word in working memory.

The more knowledge and memories we hold in our heads, the more we can take complex sensations and chunk them, 'cheating' our normal limits and enabling us to progress to more complex overall thinking and increase our general fluency.

However, where we don't have enough experience or knowledge then we cannot chunk, and our working memory can be overloaded. This is what the inexperienced driver experiences during that first driving lesson – they are unable to group together lots of familiar sensations as 'driving' as nothing is familiar. It's impossible to hold everything in their working memory at the same time.

In teacher development we often see situations where teachers' working memory is overloaded: when attempting to operate a new, unfamiliar piece of software during a challenging class; or when a beginner teacher attempts to combine classroom management with explanation and questioning.

Encoding is the process of turning short-term memories into long-term ones. Not all memories are encoded equally. The strength of the memory can be affected by many factors, including:

- which sensations or ideas seem more relevant to the task at hand;
- the intensity of our emotion at the time; and
- how hard we've worked at making meaning.

Interestingly, an explicit *intention* to try and learn something appears to have no impact on how effectively we encode it. What matters is the process of thinking used, the environment around us and where we are focusing our attention.

A series of driving lessons accompanied by regular practice should encode the sensations and experiences of driving into long-term memory.

In working with inexperienced teachers, we want them to encode a huge amount of knowledge and skill while engaging in the stressful activity of directing a whole class of students. They are naturally drawn to pay attention to the things that are most important to them, but these are not necessarily the stimuli that would be most important to an expert.

Experienced teachers sometimes must interrupt their automatic process of making sense of what they are seeing or else they end up encoding the familiar and filtering out the unfamiliar. This is what makes learning something unfamiliar so difficult – new ideas get harder to assimilate and existing thinking becomes increasingly entrenched. We also need to repeatedly encounter new or improved ideas so that they can be at least as strongly encoded as old habits and thinking. This is probably one of the reasons that effective teacher development almost always requires a sustained cycle of encountering ideas – one encounter appears to be unlikely to encode a suitably strong new pattern of thinking.

Retrieval is the process of accessing memories from long-term memory. It is mainly a pattern-matching process where the contents of working memory are matched against long-term memories to find a best fit.

Interestingly, remembering something strengthens *and* modifies the original memory. For example, if you retrieve your memory of oranges while also thinking about an unpleasant taste, then the original memory of oranges is now modified to be more associated with an unpleasant taste. Similarly, if a teacher on repeating a successful lesson finds that it now goes wrong, that teacher may then make negative associations with that content or class.

Each time you practise driving a car, you are retrieving the memory of the various sensations and tasks. Repeated practice means repeated retrieval, and this means stronger memories.

The way that retrieval works is a challenge when a teacher is trying to change the way they think about something. Every time the old, out-dated memory is triggered, it can be strengthened. It's hard to embed new ways of thinking, and hard to change old ones.

The implications

We can use this model to help understand that learning is a continuum. It is very different to engage in a task when we have very few relevant memories than to engage in that same task when we have many relevant memories. More knowledge of, and experience in, a task allows us to move from being a *novice* to gaining greater *expertise*, although there is really no limit to this level of expertise – you can pretty much always become more expert.

Someone with more expertise …

… will be familiar with most of the situations or problems they face in a particular domain. For example, an expert quadratic equation-solver will recognise the vast majority of problems as familiar and remember which strategies to try first. A teacher getting students to form a line outside the classroom can rapidly recognise and attend to a student who is not paying attention – the pattern of action and response is stored.

Someone with more expertise will be clearer on what success looks like, clearer on what the best routes to success look like and will be able to apply rapid and accurate correction if they deviate from this. For example, a dancer has a much stronger awareness of his balance, of the tension in various muscles, of where he is in contact with the floor, his momentum, etc. and this allows him to make quick corrections on the fly. A teacher of French is able to spot a common writing error with tenses and can almost effortlessly recall the best remembered options for corrective feedback.

Someone with more expertise will have better developed mental models which effectively predict and explain what is happening and which help to select alternative strategies where necessary. For example, an expert baker understands immediately why a dough feels too wet and can take informed corrective action. An expert violin teacher can identify an error with use of the bow from listening to the tone, using a clear model of how musicians develop to identify what the appropriate intervention is for this level of skill.

Finally, more expertise enables you to complete a task using less of your working memory, freeing up space for awareness of other activities or for combining multiple expert skills. For example, an expert driver can turn a corner without having to think about each element of using mirrors, using the clutch, brake and accelerator, changing gear and turning the wheel. An expert teacher can demonstrate how a piece of equipment works at the front of the class while focusing much of their attention on the reactions and mood of the class.

All these benefits require thinking, habit and practice to become 'hard coded', more automatic and deeply ingrained. This can be beneficial, but it also comes with a cost. The more that certain patterns of thinking are ingrained, the harder it is to shift them. It is not impossible, but it requires a different approach to learning if we all want to avoid being 'set in our ways'.

This means that learning something new is much harder for those who already have some expertise.

Novices …

… have no (or few) long-term memories associated with the particular task and domain. They tend to use a fairly blind application of rules or a very loose goal-seeking behaviour, making guesses at what will help them move to a 'success state'. Similarly, an inexperienced practitioner is uncertain about what a successful process or outcome looks like or how effectively they are doing.

A novice is unfamiliar with the sensations or thinking patterns of carrying out the practice. They can be easily distracted by unusual sensations, finding it harder to focus on the things that are task-critical. They are likely to be clumsy or error-prone and are less effective at diagnosing and correcting as they go. It is a lot harder to work out what to concentrate on and to filter out the unimportant. Novices are rapidly and easily overwhelmed.

A novice will not have developed mental or muscular habits/patterns associated with the task – each individual step requires more explicit thinking and concentration. Where the expert can carry out some elements of a task automatically, with little effort, a novice puts in painstaking effort to carry out even the smallest step. Novice drivers find their first, short journey exhausting and challenging.

The state of not knowing about something is not pleasant. From an evolutionary standpoint, it helped our ancestors to survive if they viewed unexpected and unexplained situations as more dangerous than familiar ones.

While not knowing something can feel stressful, we also find learning very rewarding. We have all felt the pleasurable sensation of making sense of a puzzle, of when something confusing comes into focus, of when we get a new idea that helps explain previously confusing processes.

Implications for teacher learning

Learning is a continuum and, depending on whether we are a novice in an area or whether we have some expertise, our learning will look different. The challenge then is to design teacher learning so that it deals with an ever-changing mix of both deeply ingrained thinking, when some teachers are experts, and a tendency to be overwhelmed, when they are novices.

In the intensity of the classroom, professional learning must be available for immediate use. It must be flexibly adapted to new and unexpected scenarios, applied on the fly and its results interpreted smoothly. Even when assessing and planning lessons, the time pressure is such that knowledge needs to be readily available for use – there is very little time to translate theory painstakingly into practice.

A classroom is too demanding a place to be a novice in any more than a small number of aspects. In fact, even brand-new teachers are not novices in every respect. From attending school themselves, they will have a lot of existing models and schemas for how classrooms work. Even outside the classroom, teachers do not have time to reinvent every wheel. They need to plan great lessons rapidly and efficiently and to assess effectively.

Clearly, we want to help teachers increase their level of competence in the most important and common tasks and experiences that they will encounter in the classroom. We also want to challenge areas of expertise that are outdated, incomplete or simply mistaken.

Teacher learning as a novice

An individual is neither a novice nor an expert, but will have areas or domains where they are a novice and others where they are expert. At the start of their career, teachers will have more domains which are new to them, but having been to school, they will have existing schemas, mental models and preconceptions; i.e. they have some expertise in key areas.

In those domains in which you are a novice, you have no existing models to group and clarify all that is going on in your working memory, so it is very easy to become overloaded. Structures that help teachers form simple models help them to deal with this. Worked examples, role modelling and mentoring all focus their attention on the key elements. This kind of support can be really helpful when something is completely new.

Teacher learning as an expert

Once you have some expertise in an area, it is much more difficult to set aside lessons that have already been learnt. We all have existing mental models which we use to explain and predict. To challenge one of these models implies that much of what we have thought and done will have been wrong. We all need to guard against this in case it leads us to reject new ideas and approaches.

This is nothing new.

In 1846 a young doctor, Ignaz Semmelweis, suspected that the cause of 16% infant mortality in one clinic might be the failure of doctors to wash their hands. When he ran an experiment and insisted that doctors wash hands between each patient, the deaths from fever plummeted. However, his finding ran so against the established practice and norms that his findings were not only rejected but widely mocked despite being obviously valid. This reactionary short-sightedness gave rise to the term The Semmelweis Reflex: 'the reflex-like tendency to reject new evidence or new knowledge because it contradicts established norms, beliefs or paradigms.'[4]

Sticking with what we know

One of the pitfalls here is *confirmation bias*[5] – a mental failing that means we try too hard to explain everything using our existing mental models. This leads us to dismiss, diminish or reject elements that do not fit and over-emphasise elements that do. You see this regularly in political debate – a strong supporter of one argument will see many flaws in their opponents' argument, while quietly ignoring or even denying anything good or of value. It is a failing built into how we learn and can be difficult to overcome.

For teachers, such biases can lead to superficial adoption of ideas or practice, or an incorrect assumption that what we are seeing or hearing is what we already think or do.

As we describe later in this book, one of the solutions to this issue is to ensure that teacher learning is directly linked to ongoing, robust evaluation of students' learning. This means that, even when a teacher believes that a new practice makes sense or feels better, they need to continue learning and refining it until there is a demonstrable improvement in outcomes for their students.

A second pitfall is *sunk cost bias*.[6] This is also known as the 'IKEA effect' – you're much more likely to invest in and believe in things that you have worked hard on. This is a common pitfall amongst teachers where, after spending time and effort focusing on a particular aspect of practice, they are automatically inclined to see it as successful.

Again, constantly linking back to the benefits for students and evaluative practice can help mitigate these risks. Meaningful feedback and challenge from peers can also support this. It also helps to be aware that the risk is there.

A third pitfall that makes it hard for us to change our thinking is the *Dunning–Kruger effect*.[7] This is a cognitive bias where those with just a bit of knowledge feel misplaced confidence in this knowledge and superiority, compared to those with more knowledge. In teacher learning, it is crucial to ensure that there is both exploration of the theory and experimentation in the practice of new ideas. If this experimentation is then evaluated and linked back to the student learning or expected impact, this lowers the risk of misplaced confidence in one's knowledge resulting in misguided practice.

Rejecting something new

As well as the many temptations to over-value what we already know, there are also biases which encourage us to reject anything new. Not only are we over-confident that our existing thinking can explain ideas, we tend to assume any disagreement is likely to be a character flaw in the other person. This is known as the *fundamental attribution error*.[8]

A classic example of this goes back to driving. If you accidentally make a swerve into another car, then you believe you made an honest mistake but are otherwise a good driver. If someone does the same to you, then you probably immediately assume they are a bad person, rather than assuming it was an honest mistake.

You can almost certainly recognise this in colleagues that you have worked with. In fact, typically, when we talk about biases, we find that audience members can easily recognise each bias in their colleagues. But beware also the bias blind spot – the mistaken assumption that others commonly suffer from these biases and errors while you yourself are hugely less prone. Everyone believes this. Everyone is wrong!

Fortunately, these biases are not the only psychological factors at play. Just as strong as our inclination to fool ourselves is our psychological need to form and maintain social bonds. If we are faced with an incongruous situation, then the threat of looking silly or losing face in the eyes of someone we respect and value can overcome our resistance to changing our thinking.

This means social bonds can lead to group-think. If a group reach a cosy consensus with which an outsider disagrees, it may be seen by the outsider as a flaw in their character. Equally, someone from within the group may, if they like and respect the outsider, choose to reinterpret things by saying 'what she says sounds wrong, but actually I think that we are both right because…'

Another variation is the *Halo Effect*,[9] where you are much less likely to doubt statements made by someone you respect. The reverse is that we are likely to excessively doubt statements made by someone we dislike.

It might happen more subtly than this. As we discuss new ideas with colleagues, we are likely to view respected colleagues' ideas more charitably and be less likely to question them deeply, instead choosing to encourage and praise.

On the other hand, this powerful social impulse can also be used to break group-think. If a respected expert and professional comes to work with a group of teachers then, as long as the relationship is maintained, the desire to impress the expert can break the cycle of group-think and offer a route into entirely new thinking.

> *Powerful professional development tends to be a bit disruptive and a bit uncomfortable. While it is easy to veneer existing practice with a shiny new approach, powerful professional learning takes place in the core – in beliefs, mental models and expectations.*

The expert, from outside our usual group, is able to offer a brand-new perspective on what may be familiar issues. They can give more convincing explanations that help to address teachers' concerns more effectively than pre-existing mental models. They can present just enough challenging information to disrupt existing thinking without causing teachers to retreat into their comfort zone or get hostile.

> Successful facilitators build a relationship with participants that allows them to share values, understanding, goals and beliefs with participants, while providing important challenge at the same time.

(Cordingley et al. 2015)[10]

Confirmation bias	We try too hard to explain everything using our existing mental models, leading us to dismiss, diminish or reject elements that don't fit and over-emphasise elements that do.
Sunk cost bias	You're much more likely to invest in and believe in things that you have worked hard on.
Dunning–Kruger effect	Those with just a bit of knowledge feel misplaced confidence and superiority in this knowledge compared to those with more knowledge.
Fundamental attribution error	We tend to assume any disagreement is likely to be a character flaw in the other person.
Halo Effect	We are much less likely to doubt statements made by someone we respect. The reverse is that we are likely to excessively doubt statements made by someone we dislike.

Summary

Learning is hard. Learning as a teacher, with all the inherent challenges of the classroom, staffroom and working with young people, is even harder. There are innate biases encouraging us to stick with what we know and reject new learning. Not only that, sometimes there is a pressure to know what you're doing to the point that identifying what you don't know is implicitly discouraged.

Some people see teaching as a vocation or that good teachers are 'born and not made'. What that hides are how many different aspects of good teaching there are, and how a teacher's practice constantly needs to be adapted to meet the needs of the students in front of them. A key part of professional learning is seeing it as continuous and constant. You will be a 'novice' in some aspects of your practice, an 'expert' in others for the length of your career.

To overcome this, we need to be aware of our innate biases. We need to ensure that there are opportunities to engage with expertise that will disrupt our thinking and we need to be aware of and open to new evidence and research challenging our thinking. We need to rigorously link our learning and practice to the impact on students, and ensure we use meaningful feedback and evaluative practices to support this. By engaging in learning that is rooted in evidence-informed theory and in our own contexts and practice, we can avoid some of these pitfalls.

In this book, we summarise ideas from research and practice that are helping schools to do this and to create much more effective professional learning.

Further reading

Fernandez, E. (n.d.). A Visual Study Guide to Cognitive Biases – https://www.scribd.com/doc/30548590/Cognitive-Biases-A-Visual-Study-Guide

Clark, R. E., Kirschner, P. A., & Sweller, J. (2012). Putting Students on the Path to Learning – an American Educator article on key ideas about memory and learning from cognitive science. https://www.aft.org/sites/default/files/periodicals/Clark.pdf

Notes

1 Sweller, J. (1988). Cognitive load during problem solving: Effects on learning. *Cognitive Science*, 12: 257–285. doi:10.1207/s15516709cog1202_4

2 Atkinson, R. C., & Shiffrin, R. M. (1968). Human memory: A proposed system and its control processes. In Spence, K. W., & Spence, J. T. *The Psychology of Learning and Motivation* (Volume 2). New York: Academic Press. pp. 89–195.

3 Atkinson, R. C., & Shiffrin, R. M. (1968). Chapter: Human memory: A proposed system and its control processes. In Spence, K. W., & Spence, J. T. *The Psychology of Learning and Motivation* (Volume 2). New York: Academic Press. pp. 89–195.

4 'Ignaz Semmelweis' (2017) in *Wikipedia: The Free Encyclopedia*, Wikimedia Foundation Inc., viewed on 19 November 2017. https://en.wikipedia.org/wiki/Ignaz_Semmelweis

5 Eysenck, M. W.,; & Keane, M. T. (2010). *Cognitive Psychology: A Student's Handbook*, 6th Edition (Kindle Location 8389). Taylor & Francis. Kindle Edition.

6 Arkes, H. R., & Ayton, P. (1999). The sunk cost and Concorde effects: Are humans less rational than lower animals? *Psychological Bulletin*, 125(5): 591–600. http://dx.doi.org/10.1037/0033-2909.125.5.591

7 Kruger, J., & Dunning, D. (1999). Unskilled and unaware of it: How difficulties in recognizing one's own incompetence lead to inflated self-assessments. *Journal of Personality and Social Psychology. American Psychological Association*, 77(6): 1121–1134. CiteSeerX 10.1.1.64.2655 Freely accessible. doi:10.1037/0022-3514.77.6.1121

8 Ross, L. (1977). The intuitive psychologist and his shortcomings: Distortions in the attribution process. In Berkowitz, L. *Advances in Experimental Social Psychology*. New York: Academic Press. pp. 173–220.

9 'The Halo Effect' (2017). in *Wikipedia: The Free Encyclopedia*, Wikimedia Foundation Inc., viewed on 19 November 2017. https://en.wikipedia.org/wiki/Halo_effect

10 Cordingley, P., Higgins, S., Greany, T., Buckler, N., Coles-Jordan, D., Crisp, B., Saunders, L., & Coe, R. (2015). Developing great teaching: Lessons from the international reviews into effective professional development. *Teacher Development Trust*. http://TDTrust.org/about/dgt

two
The purpose of professional learning
A framework of outcomes

Our key priority is helping teachers learn so that they can more effectively teach their students. Unleashing great teaching through great professional learning not only helps improve outcomes for students, but it helps teachers thrive.

We want to help create a 'golden thread' from designing learning activities for staff members through to better student learning in classrooms. As we have just explored, a closer focus on the impact on students enables us to avoid many of our innate biases. We believe that it is vital to keep checking how our professional learning helps our students succeed.

We have found that school leaders find designing professional learning that is focused on the organisational edge is easier when thinking about a framework of outcomes. This framework helps identify the nature of the intended impact from professional learning and the depth of expertise that is needed. These outcomes should then be planned for across a professional learning programme.

Activities versus programmes

It can be helpful to draw a distinction between professional learning *activities* and *programmes*.

- **Activity**: an individual process, activity, session or event.
- **Programme**: a coherent series of activities and opportunities which combine to produce an effective, sustained professional learning outcome.

For example, spending a day listening to expert speakers about developing coaching techniques at an external conference venue is a one-off *activity*. By itself, it may have limited impact: there is little time to encode the learning or explore how it can work in your own context. However, it could be part of a year-long *programme* of professional learning developed to support the transition of staff into leadership roles.

Before the day, participants could engage in self-review to understand their own existing thinking and attitudes. They could work in a small group to explore challenges in school coaching, identifying a few key members of staff who will be the initial intended beneficiaries of the programme to help understand the challenge. On the day, participants can now ask relevant questions and find tools that directly relate to their particular context and barriers. In the following days and weeks, the small group can work together to plan and implement approaches, bringing in selected experts to work with them.

We would broadly encourage schools and school leaders to think more in terms of designing *programmes* of professional learning and then select helpful activities within this.

Intended impact

Schools are sizeable organisations and the list of development priorities can be endless. The busier that schools are, the more important it is to have clarity about the intended impact of each activity.

The first thing to consider in the framework of outcomes is the nature of the intended impact. The most important consideration for a professional learning programme is how will it benefit students, and how we will know whether it has benefitted students. In doing so, we make a distinction which draws on ideas from England's Standard for Teachers' Professional Development.[1]

Direct impact	Targeted at specific benefits for students, i.e. focused on impact at the organisational edge.
Indirect impact	Designed to support teams and organisation to function more effectively so that, ultimately, students benefit, i.e. focused on improving the organisation's capacity to support direct impact.

We want to be clear from the outset that we define benefits and outcomes for students broadly. While it does encompass grades and certificates achieved in formal examinations, we also include:

- narrower outcomes such as deep understanding of specific concepts; and
- non-academic, broader outcomes such as wellbeing, ability to contribute to society, ability to discover and utilise one's own talents, opportunity to gain meaningful employment or start a new enterprise.

Direct impact

For many professional learning activities and programmes, it is possible to trace the thread right through to the desired impact on students at the organisational edge. Specifically, it should be possible for participants to identify specific students and evaluate whether their professional learning is having an impact on these students. We find it is sometimes helpful to include the words 'SO AS' or 'SO THAT' as a way to ensure that the benefit to students is explicitly stated.

Examples

- *A series of workshops on improving classroom feedback SO AS to help students who are struggling with an aspect of mathematics, evaluated through repeatedly observing how pupils are tackling series of short problems.*

- *A programme of meetings to develop a new series of learning activities and lessons (as part of an updated science curriculum) SO AS to improve understanding of key scientific concepts, evaluated through tests, focusing on those students who have previously expressed interest in studying science later in life.*
- *A series of one-to-one coaching and observation activities to help a teacher improve behaviour management SO AS to eliminate most disruptive incidents in a Year 4 reading class, evaluated through observations of behaviour, student surveys and formal behaviour records.*

There is a clear, intended outcome and a logical connection between each activity and the intended outcome and evaluation.

For a professional learning programme to be *direct*, it is not enough to simply design an activity to improve teaching in the hope that student attainment improves as a result. An hour-long training session on how to ask better questions is unlikely to qualify as having direct impact if participants are not clear on which students they are supposed to be specifically helping, nor how they'd know if the professional learning was having the intended impact.

It is easy to see, however, that the one-hour activity on how to ask better questions *could* contribute to the first and second examples above. As part of a programme to improve feedback to those struggling with maths or to improve understanding of scientific concepts amongst those interested in science, asking better questions might have an important role.

Indirect impact

Some activities and programmes are designed to develop and improve the organisation and the staff. The organisational centre needs to ensure success at the edge. These are enabling activities that improve the ability of teachers to have direct impact on their students.

Indirect activities could include leadership development, training in emergency procedures or systems. Each of these should help the organisation run more effectively so that the organisation can succeed and improve.

Examples

- *A training session to help school staff members to use an online behaviour recording system SO THAT the organisation is able to more rapidly identify and respond to behaviour issues and provide support to the relevant staff and students.*
- *A development programme to support staff in middle leadership positions to develop management and leadership skills SO THAT teams are able to focus more effectively on improving students' learning.*

The key part of designing an activity with indirect impact is to be clear how it helps individuals, teams and the organisation function more effectively so that teaching, learning and direct-impact professional learning can have greater impact.

Indirect activities could also aim to bring in new knowledge and awareness into the organisation. They are aimed at addressing the question, 'what is it that we don't know that we don't know?'

The aim is to provide ingredients for future learning and development, to inspire ideas, to connect the organisation to thinking in the wider system.

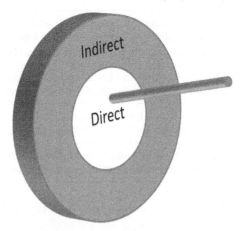

FIGURE 2.1   Bulls-eye: it's important to ensure that enough professional learning activities are aimed at direct impact.

Examples

- *Spending a day at a large education conference to see and to hear about the latest developments in education technology SO THAT professional learning is informed by them.*
- *Staying up to date with the latest pedagogical discussions using social media SO THAT we are aware of the latest principles and can investigate them further.*
- *Visiting a nearby school which has a reputation for exceptionally successful teaching practice SO THAT I can be inspired and raise my expectations of what is possible to achieve in my own professional learning.*

Balancing direct and indirect

Teachers and schools are there for public service: to help students succeed in their learning and life. This suggests that the balance of professional learning activities in most schools needs to be focused on programmes and activities that have direct impact. It is a good check to review how much time is being spent on indirect-impact professional learning, compared to direct-impact (Figure 2.1).

Depth

The second section of the framework of outcomes is the depth of expertise required. As explored in the previous chapter, learning is complicated and we want to develop experts who are able to apply and adapt different lessons learnt to their practice. Developing practice that will directly benefit students will require a lot more work than developing background awareness.

The table below can help when designing professional learning activities and programmes. Not every piece of professional learning will neatly fit, but we find it helpful as a thinking aid even if there is some overlap between categories.

Adaptive practice	High level of expertise, automaticity and ability to apply flexibly. The hardest to achieve but also, despite being flexible to different circumstances, the hardest practice to change once embedded.
Deliberative practice	Expert practice that can be carried out flexibly with some supports and with time to carefully think through each step.
Procedural practice	Proficient practice that fairly rigidly follows a set procedure or set of rules without significant ability to vary or adapt.
Awareness	A background awareness of the existence of certain ideas without sufficient clarity or depth to yet crystallise into practice.

When a teacher is in a classroom, she doesn't have time to stop and weigh up different approaches, to consult a guidebook or to get out a checklist to follow. She needs to know enough underlying theory to make smart decisions and to adapt that theory on the fly.

Above all, given the complexity of the classroom, this particular practice must not take up all of her attention and working memory. She needs to be able to take a practice and use it expertly, automatically, and flexibly, integrating it into the many other things that she is doing.

Similarly, when a leader is faced with an unexpected difficult conversation with a colleague, she also doesn't have time to stop and weigh up different options. She also needs to use practice expertly and fluently.

This is what we'd call **adaptive** practice. It is both the hardest to achieve and also the hardest to change once embedded. It requires a high level of expertise and automaticity.

On the other hand, when a teacher is in the staffroom planning a lesson, she needs to do so efficiently but is able to stop and consult advice. She doesn't necessarily need to have internalised all of the necessary knowledge although she will certainly need to be sufficiently familiar with it to avoid being overwhelmed and to efficiently pick out the elements that she needs.

This is what we'd call **deliberative** practice. It still requires the internalising of sufficient examples and the theory of how to vary and adapt them effectively. It requires an understanding of where to go to find advice.

In some cases, all that is required is for a member of staff to reproduce a list of actions. This could be following a simple evacuation procedure, learning to complete the steps required to enter a piece of data into an IT system or knowing some basic rules of what to do if there is a fire alarm. In most of these cases the member of staff is expected to rely on others' expertise but ensure that the correct procedure is followed until that expert gets involved.

This is what we'd call **procedural** practice.

In other cases, it is helpful for teachers to simply have an awareness of ideas, theories and practices without a need to reproduce them. This is typically helpful background **awareness** which builds knowledge and thinking for later, deeper learning.

What does this mean for professional learning?

These key outcomes and levels of depth can be helpful when considering the intended impact and purpose of their professional learning.

Below are some key questions to ask:

1. What is the balance? Teachers will typically need to work primarily on developing adaptive and deliberative practice – but there is a place too for awareness and for procedural practice.

   Example 1 *A teacher of five years' experience might be engaged in developing his management skills through a leadership programme. This will likely have **indirect impact** on his students as it is intended to support team and organisational effectiveness. He will need to develop **adaptive expertise** in these management skills, so that he can respond effectively while in one-to-one meetings and team meetings. He may need support to design opportunities for his team to engage in professional learning discussions with **direct impact**, intended to build their own **adaptive expertise**.*

   Example 2 *A middle leader spends much of her allocated professional learning time on visiting other schools and attending subject association conferences. This builds her **background awareness** and leaves her inspired with lots of ideas, but has not **directly benefitted** students yet. She needs to have time and resource to turn these ideas and inspiration into practice.*

2. What type of professional learning processes do we need? For building adaptive practice, more sustained opportunities are required, with chances to experiment, build and embed everyday practice. Whereas to develop deliberative knowledge, procedural knowledge or awareness, the professional learning processes can be much simpler.

   Example 1 *Students often underperform in their writing assessments compared to their reading assessments. A team of teachers are focused on developing writing, focused on a few key aspects of writing. This will require a sustained and effective professional learning programme to develop their **adaptive practice**.*

   Example 2 *There have been significant changes to an exam specification. Teachers will need to develop an **awareness** of the changes needed, and then their **deliberative expertise** to plan or amend schemes of work accordingly. They will then need to develop their **adaptive practice** as they become more experienced and skilled at teaching new areas.*

3. How will you ensure that professional learning is meeting your students', staff's and school's needs? Being really clear and specific about the expected impact ensures that your professional learning is well planned for needs, but also supports you in evaluating the impact of any learning that takes place.

   Example 1 *A senior leader hoping to become a Headteacher may invest time into her leadership skills, which **indirectly** benefit students, but will hopefully also be refining and improving her **adaptive practice**.*

   Example 2 *The leaders of a science department with very few physics specialists might need to develop **awareness** of key pedagogical strategies through general background reading – an activity with **indirect impact** so that they can start developing **procedural practice** in the classroom to enable some teaching basics to be put in place, moving on to **deliberative practice**, and ultimately **adaptive practice**.*

The next chapter explores this framework further by unpicking the evaluation of professional learning, constantly linking any learning back to the expected impact and ultimate benefit to students.

Note

1   Weston et al. (2016). Standard for Teachers' Professional Development, *Department for Education.* https://www.gov.uk/government/publications/standard-for-teachers-professional-development

three
Impact
Implementing and evaluating professional learning

Why is the evaluation of professional learning important?

Professional learning benefits students and teachers. It helps the school meet its development priorities. Designed well, it should empower and enable success at the organisational edge, supporting everyone to best meet student, parent and community needs.

Yet it's all too easy to design and facilitate ineffective professional learning and we have probably all taken part in sessions that may even have been enjoyable and interesting but that were not effective. Teaching is a demanding job; it is imperative that professional learning has impact.

Designing professional learning for impact – and measuring that impact – is much more difficult. The framework of outcomes identified in the previous chapter should help to structure and define impact, but reality is complicated and what looks clear at a theoretical level can be hard to implement in practice. This chapter seeks to break down the evaluation of professional learning, both at teacher and leadership level. There are also examples of how to structure and facilitate effective professional learning.

Our aim in this book is to stop evaluation being seen as separate from professional learning. Professional learning should be *responsive*, not merely delivered and parroted (Figure 3.1). It needs to develop genuine expertise by *evaluative practitioners* who are constantly checking for impact.

We begin by explaining how to design professional learning programmes to achieve different depths of impact. We then move on to more detailed exploration of professional learning design to get *deliberative* or *adaptive* levels of expertise. This is called *Responsive Professional Learning* and we explore each stage and how you can structure and support it.

Finally, we review effective evaluation of a whole programme – the birds-eye view of impact.

Designing for depth of impact

When designing a professional learning programme, consider two key factors.

FIGURE 3.1 Professional learning shouldn't merely be delivered and parroted, it needs to be responsive.

1. The prior knowledge, skill and experience of participants – where are they on the *novice → expert* continuum? i.e. how much previous experience, thinking and practice are they bringing to the table?
2. The intended depth of impact – what is the intended level of expertise?

As we described in Chapter Two, people who have very little experience and very little existing thinking in a topic learn differently to those who have more existing or entrenched ideas. For processes aimed mainly at teachers with less experience in a practice, an effective professional learning programme will include more worked examples, demonstrations or models of the practice/skill being learned. You need to gradually build up the mental *schema* with plenty of concrete examples.

For processes aimed at those with more existing experience and expertise, an effective professional learning programme should include more opportunities for participants to explore and experiment. Participants need opportunities to see how reality is different to what they expect to allow them to change existing thinking patterns.

However, changing practice isn't straightforward. It's easy for participants to feel uncomfortable or even angry when their existing thinking is challenged. Effective professional learning requires careful facilitation with high levels of trust. Facilitators need to help participants see things in new ways without activating internal biases that would cause them to entirely reject or to only selectively accept elements of the new ideas.

The greater the depth of expertise required, the longer the programme needs to last. This is in order to give more opportunities to try practising and adapting the ideas in different situations, and to learn how to integrate the practice with other thinking.

		Pre-existing knowledge, skill	
		No or very few existing ideas and preconceptions $\rightarrow$	Entrenched existing practice/ideas
Depth of expertise sought	Awareness & inspiration	One-off input may be sufficient	
	Procedural knowledge	Multiple chances to observe, practise and get feedback	
	Deliberative expertise		Increasing level of experimentation needed, more sustained, more collaboration and dialogue helpful.
	Adaptive expertise		Extended enquiry approach over time with plenty of expert challenge

- To achieve *awareness* participants typically require only brief exposure to ideas. An example might be listening to a talk, reading a blog or watching a demonstration.
- *Procedural knowledge* is developed through rehearsal. Examples might include practising the procedure to follow during a fire alarm, how to recalibrate an interactive whiteboard or how to record a behaviour incident on a computer system. Each process might be described or demonstrated first, then attempted by participants with some basic feedback from someone with greater expertise.

  Changing or improving existing procedural expertise may require some slightly more intense and careful work to identify what needs to change, then enough practice of the new approach until it is a stronger memory than the old approach. This is not necessarily straightforward. It's easy to imagine someone forgetting which version of a procedure to use when under stress.

- Developing *deliberative expertise* for novices typically begins with procedural expertise (i.e. practising simple examples) and then understanding how to adjust the approach to suit a variety of different challenges and contexts. An example could be learning to use a mark scheme in the assessment of an exam paper. Working through multiple examples and getting feedback from an expert, the teacher gradually develops expertise and understanding about the underlying principles.

  Changing the deliberative expertise of experts is more difficult. It's dangerously easy to adopt superficial changes to practice without challenging and changing underlying thinking. An example could be the use of lesson outcomes in planning. It's fairly easy to superficially add an outcome at the beginning of every lesson, but it's quite a different thing to approach your planning with a clear focus on the intended outcomes and to select and plan every activity accordingly. It is then an *adaptive* skill to take this thinking into the classroom and to adapt your lesson according to how well students meet your intended outcomes.

- As every new teacher has discovered, developing *adaptive expertise* in the classroom is the most difficult learning challenge. There are so many strands of practice and thinking that need to be integrated, from remembering how to conduct explanations and questioning, through building rapport with students while fostering effective behaviour, to dealing with classroom furniture, computer systems and practical constraints of time, equipment and space. While all of this is happening, the teacher needs to be aware of her voice, body language and movement around the classroom, mindful of how she is presenting ideas on a board, and always aware of the body language and mood of individual students and the overall class community.

If learning new practices is hard, then changing an existing adaptive practice is harder still. Try to keep a lesson running smoothly while trying to consciously override an existing habit or pattern of thought – that's extremely difficult.

The development of deliberative and adaptive expertise tends to require the most careful design. We explore this further in this next section.

The Responsive Professional Learning (RPL) cycle

Professional learning for *adaptive* and *deliberative* expertise requires a carefully designed process in order to overcome biases, change habits and develop expertise. Typically speaking, teachers will need to engage with an idea more than once in order to sustainably change their thinking and practice.

Professional learning is often represented as straightforward cycle. However, we feel that it's better represented as *Responsive Professional Learning*, or *RPL*, a cycle with small loops within a large loop, as shown in Figure 3.2.

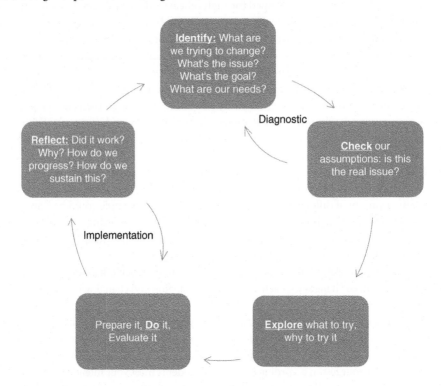

FIGURE 3.2   The Responsive Professional Learning Cycle.

Key ideas

1. Start with the intended impact in mind: clarify how the learning will impact on others rather than focusing only on perfecting a practice.
2. Check assumptions and diagnose the real barriers.
3. Ensure that participants are *evaluative* – constantly checking the impact their learning is having on others.
4. Complex ideas and practices are learned over time – build in multiple opportunities to try, evaluate and reflect on progress.

Core ingredients

There are a number of important principles for the entire cycle.

First, the process is typically more effective when participants collaborate to solve the problem – not just as a brief one-off, but over a sustained period of time. This encourages them to articulate thinking and stimulates debate. It also allows mutual support when things get challenging and mutual accountability to keep the process on track and on time. It ensures that they engage with ideas more than once, forming stronger memories and embedding new habits.

Second, the process should take place within a culture where participants feel supported to learn and explore new thinking. We discuss this aspect more in Chapter Four, 'Culture: the make or break for professional learning'.

Finally, the process requires external expertise, quality leadership and careful facilitation.

- Expertise: someone who has more knowledge and experience of the problem being solved and the approach being tried. As explored in Chapter Five, it is useful for this person to be from outside the institution or team.
- Leadership: a senior practitioner or leader who can work to find and protect resources for the group, manage competing pressures, champion findings and bring the bigger picture priorities into the group.
- Facilitation: someone with experience of the Responsive Professional Learning process who can induct and guide participants through the process. The facilitator can help with timings, collecting evidence and with maintaining the structure of the overall process and the individual discussions. They can also help to co-ordinate the work of expert and leader, while potentially sharing ideas and findings between groups with similar goals.

This next section explores the stages of Responsive Professional Learning in further detail: identify and check; explore; prepare, do and evaluate; and reflect and sustain.

Identify and check: the diagnostic process

Too often, evaluation is considered at the end of a professional learning process. It is tempting to pursue an interesting idea and retrospectively check if it is working or has worked.

However, to know *whether* something has worked and *how* it has worked, you need a good understanding of:

- the baseline – what you started with;
- the focus – the need you are seeking to address; and
- the goal – what success looks like.

A good diagnostic process starts with a clear and specific understanding of what you are seeking to achieve or change. With that clarity, identifying that change becomes much easier.

Identifying the aims

If you ask a teacher 'what *one thing* would you really like to improve, change or work on this year with one of your classes?', they are, in our experience, likely to come back with a quick answer. Identifying a broad need or concern is normally not difficult. For example, 'I wish I could better challenge my high prior-attaining students' or 'I wish I could improve their literacy'. Whilst these are admirable aims, they are also very general ones with a number of possible ways in which they could be addressed.

The diagnostic process helps participants to clarify their intentions. It's a process of triangulating ideas, perspectives and evidence.

Key questions for **identifying** a focus

1. What will look different if we are successful?
2. What barriers do we need to overcome, and why?
3. What strengths are we bringing and what challenges are we facing with this task?

Key questions for **checking** our assumptions

1. Have we identified the right factor to achieve success? Is it the most important issue to look at right now?
2. How can we test whether we've identified the right barriers to success?
3. Is our vision of success appropriate, clear and achievable?
4. Are we really clear about our existing strengths and challenges?

The identifying phase is about gaining clarity. It ensures that participants and facilitators are really clear about the current problem, the change they want to make and the underpinning theories that explain it.

Here's an example of an aim: 'the one thing I would like is more challenge for my high-attaining students'. By itself, this aim is a little fuzzy. We'd want to pose several questions:

- What is the current level of challenge for high-attainers? Do you have some kind of measure or baseline?
- What should 'more challenge' look like? How would we know if it was happening successfully?
- Why is it needed? If the aim is higher scores in exams, then is lack of challenge really the main issue, or is it something else, or a combination of factors?
- Why isn't it happening now – what's the barrier? Is more challenge the right solution for all of the students we're considering, or only for some?
- What do we already know about challenge? Have any of us tried this before? What do we feel about this? Do we know where to find out more? Are we *really* accurately assessing our own knowledge and existing skill?

There are several important perspectives to take into account when identifying and clarifying an aim.

Teachers and support staff who work with children are the ones who spend the most time at the organisational edge. They have the largest number of interactions with students, parents and the community, and they are the ones who are most engaged in student learning and supporting successful student outcomes.

Students themselves provide vital perspectives. Teaching is a process of effecting change in a student's head. There's so much rich information to help teachers when they engage students in a dialogue about their own learning. Similarly, students' friends and family can be fascinating sources of information about how their learning is going.

Expert practitioners and researchers come with an additional perspective. They are likely to have seen many examples of success and failure, and they bring richer mental models about how and why teaching and learning can be successful. They may be able to identify a key opportunity or barrier that may not be obvious to those with less experience.

Too often, we see professional learning processes where priorities are set only by senior leaders based on small snapshots of performance and highly aggregated test data. While leaders' perspectives are important, using only this isolated perspective and failing to engage teachers themselves can result in professional learning that misses important priorities.

Checking assumptions

Once a focus has been identified, it is tempting to jump straight into action. Of course we want to address the issue straightaway and go with the momentum that has already been generated, but the danger is that this can lead to naïve assumptions being made about barriers and solutions, or a failure to really challenge thinking which leads to sticking-plaster learning.

The **checking** phase is a vital 'pause for breath' before taking action. It counters our natural enthusiasm and enables us to avoid putting valuable effort into a superficial solution.

Example 1

Three teachers at Cherry Tree Primary are trying to improve their students' independent learning skills. They say that the aim is, 'to get our students to work more independently' and that the barrier is 'they don't know the strategies for working independently'. When asked how they will evaluate success, they suggest that students would get on with tasks more quickly and need less guidance – this will be measured via video clips.

The professional learning leader asks them to check their assumptions. She asks: are you sure about your assumption that it's a lack of strategies for working independently that is causing students to need so much guidance before getting on with tasks in the classroom? Could it be something else?

Once this question is posed, the teachers plan an activity to check their assumptions. They plan to:

- use a survey to try and elicit their students' understanding of independent learning strategies;
- record some short video clips of their class while a variety of different tasks are introduced, over the course of a few lessons; and
- conduct some brief interviews with students to ask them to explain the way they worked.

After gathering their survey data and video clips they meet again with the professional learning leader. To their surprise, some of the students who are able to name several strategies were among those who still needed the most guidance to get started. Their interview notes and video clips lead them to a conclusion that in some of the cases the teacher needed to explain the task more clearly, while in other cases the teacher needed to more clearly signpost self-help resources for students to use.

This short diagnostic cycle enabled them to avoid jumping straight in to teach independent learning strategies. It helped them understand the real barriers in their class and meant that their solution was more targeted and useful.

Example 2

At Dennington High School, senior leaders identified a group of students who were consistently underperforming in their exams. These students were the ones who achieved the highest scores in their primary school exams.

The leaders' initial instinct is that this is because the students have not been asked sufficiently challenging higher-order questions by their teachers. Before launching into a programme of professional learning around higher-order questions, the leaders engage in a checking phase.

They assume that if the problem is a lack of higher-order questions then they should see more progress in this cohort of students in the classrooms of teachers who are asking more of these questions. They also expect that a nearby school which makes more progress with this cohort should have a much greater number of higher order questions visible in their lessons.

The leaders work with a small team of teachers to watch higher-attaining students in different classes. They invite in teachers from another school that get much higher level of attainment for similar students. They take some of their school's teachers to observe lessons at the other school to explore whether higher order questioning appears to be the key issue.

Finally, they bring together all of their observations. It is clear that higher order questioning is different between the two schools, though more in nature than in quantity. They find that other factors appear to be just as significant: the amount of low-level disruption, the quality of vocabulary and spoken communication and the expectations of the number of practice questions and activities completed during class and for homework.

As a result of this work, teachers and leaders are clearer about the changes they would like to make. They have a better idea of what success looks like, and of a range of factors that they need to address to achieve it. The teachers, having engaged in the diagnostic cycle, are more engaged in solving the problem and feel more confident that the proposed solution is fit-for-purpose.

The diagnostic cycle of identifying and checking is useful in a number of situations.

- When teachers define their professional learning priorities for the year ahead.
- As the first stage of engaging in a Responsive Professional Learning model (e.g. collaborative enquiry, Lesson Study, etc.)
- Before or during engagement with external expertise. Participants should start a professional learning activity with real clarity around what students need and how this professional learning activity might ultimately help them.

The following sets of questions may be helpful to support the identification and clarification of professional learning priorities.

Qualities and characteristics

What kind of qualities do you want your students to have by the time they leave your school?

What kind of qualities would enable your students to be successful learners while they are in your school?

What gaps do you see between these aspirations and how students actually develop? Why are these gaps occurring? Which students are more likely to fall into them?

Development goals

What are your current school/phase/department/faculty/team development goals and priorities?

What are the gaps between these aspirations for students and the current reality? What are the reasons for these gaps? Which students are more likely to have these issues?

What are your priorities within the curriculum?

What are the gaps in the curriculum between aspiration and reality? Which part of the curriculum do students regularly struggle with?

Data

What student strengths and weaknesses are revealed by test and exam data? Why?

What student strengths and weaknesses are revealed by behavioural records and observations? Why?

What choices are your students making after studying with you? Do they engage in further study and are they being successful elsewhere?

What do the data tell us about which students have issues to address and which have strengths that could be developed?

Pupil and teacher goals and interests

What learning needs and aspirations do pupils have? Is there a gap between the current reality and these aspirations? If so, why?

Are there any areas of pupil learning that you are particularly interested in or feel particularly strongly about?

Are there any pupils who have identified themselves as needing extra attention? Have colleagues expressed an interest in supporting any particular groups?

Decision time

I will focus on the following students_____,

who currently have the following need _____.

If I'm successful in meeting their needs, instead of seeing_____,

I will see_____ in my lesson

and in their work.

Tips for picking an effective focus for a professional learning cycle

- *Do* make sure that you are clear about the students you will focus upon. Which group needs your attention? What makes them similar? What makes them different?
- *Do* make sure that you address an issue that you find challenging and important.
- *Do* try and pick a focus that will be helpful to other colleagues, if you can. You can then collaborate and share practice, especially if it links to a team, department or whole-school development plan.

- *Avoid* goals based on teacher behaviour or teaching method, e.g. 'improve behaviour management', 'make better use of Assessment for Learning' – these belong in the 'how to address the issue' phase, not in diagnosing student needs.
- *Avoid* broad data-focused goals, e.g. 'all students should achieve at least a C-grade'. This is less motivating and only superficially addresses the *actual learning* going on – what concepts, topics, skills and knowledge do students need to learn better in order to increase their attainment? Data can inform your diagnostic process, especially when you break overall grades or scores down into individual tasks or questions.
- *Avoid* laundry lists, e.g. 'Students will master basic skills and become independent learners while also developing their self-motivation and confidence'.
- *Consider* how measurable your goals are. You will want to create a package of assessments and evaluation tools to check on the progress you are making and demonstrate efficacy to other colleagues. Do you need a baseline assessment to compare against?

For teachers who bring significant experience or existing thinking: provide examples of well-identified goals and barriers to help participants structure their own thinking. Constructively challenge participants to be clear about their goals. You don't have to challenge every incorrect assumption, especially for more experienced staff – it may occasionally be more effective to let them follow a strongly held assumption through the process and discover for themselves that there are other perspectives.

For leaders/facilitators: leave space for diagnostic work at the start of any professional learning programme. Maintain a balance of encouraging the checking of assumptions without squashing enthusiasm or slowing down a process so much that teachers lose interest. Show others that you check your own assumptions and biases.

In our Chapter Six we explore more fully the process of whole-school needs analysis to create an overall professional learning plan.

Explore the issue

At this stage in the process, participants have gained some clarity around what they want to achieve, where they're starting from, what the barriers are and how they will evaluate impact.

The next step is to identify what to learn: the practices and theories that are most likely to help. Seeking the right approach to try requires both ingenuity and scholarship. Ingenuity is required because classrooms are complex and dynamic – the right solution has to fit students, staff and the school. Scholarship is required to systematically find what is already known and help us determine what is most likely to work best.

If a teacher is trying to improve the fluency of her students' reading, she needs to draw on:

- what she already knows,
- what she knows that she's aware of but doesn't fully understand and
- unknowns – ideas that she wasn't previously aware of and can seek systematically.

The trouble is, our judgements about our own knowledge may well be inaccurate. We make sense of the world based on what we know, but that doesn't mean that we've formed a correct or balanced picture. As we discussed in Chapter One, the Dunning–Kruger[1] effect is ever-present: the frequent and incorrect assumption that we know more about something than we really do.

The assumptions that we make, the experiences that we bring with us; these all guide us to cherry-pick the most comfortable ideas and practices rather than those that are necessarily the most helpful.

We explore the process of seeking expertise and research evidence more fully in Chapter Five. This input is important for:

- identifying potentially helpful approaches to try;
- learning about possible barriers to success;
- finding high-quality tools and approaches that can assess impact with reasonable reliability and validity;
- suggesting other related factors that need exploring; and
- providing important information about the pros and cons and the 'how' and 'why' of an approach.

Here are some key principles for seeking expertise and evidence:

1. Carefully review your context to help you select the expertise. There are four key factors to explore when finding the right approach and these need to be synthesised together carefully:
   a. Practitioner judgement and experience – drawing existing perspectives.
   b. Practitioner preferences and values – identifying factors that make adoption easier or harder.
   c. The context: culture, pressures and plans of a team, organisation and the wider system – identifying surrounding factors that could support or challenge adoption.
   d. Research and evaluation – identifying systematic evidence of credibly successful approaches.
2. Seek knowledge and perspective from outside of your setting. External input is enormously helpful to provide new ways to see old problems, or to uncover hidden issues. Experts play a vital role in translating practice from elsewhere into something workable in your context. They can also summarise and explain key research findings.
3. Choose a well-evidenced approach. An expert should be able to provide more than anecdotal evidence about their approach. Schools need to exercise caution when selecting expert input. Prioritise those with well-evidenced and evaluated successes, rather than reputation or personal relationships.
4. Remember that all research evidence is not equal. Seek systematic reviews of the full range of research in a field, where possible. Avoid relying on one-off studies, no matter how exciting or comforting their findings. Use Daniel Willingham's 4 steps to verify claims,[2] which he describes as:
   a. *Strip it. Clear away the verbiage and look at the actual claim. What exactly is the claim suggesting a teacher or parent should do, and what outcome is promised?*
   b. *Trace it. Who created this idea, and what have others said about it? It is common to believe something because an authority confirms it, and this is often a reasonable thing to do. I think people rely heavily on credentials when evaluating education research, but I argue that it's a weak indicator of truth.*
   c. *Analyse it. Why are you being asked to believe the claim is true? What evidence is offered, and how does the claim square with your own experience?*

d.   *Should I do it? You're not going to adopt every educational program that is scientifically backed, and it may make sense to adopt one that has not been scientifically evaluated.*

Daniel Willingham, 'When Can You Trust the Experts?'

Participants need to engage with evidence and expertise. In practice, this may be through direct engagement with research literature, it may be identified through research summaries, a blog, or a colleague's expertise, or it may be through engaging with an external expert who can facilitate evidence-informed approaches.

A teacher can learn a piece of new information but it will not become a meaningful part of their practice unless they are given time and support to embed it into their practice and, crucially, they see that it benefits their students. A key part of turning evidence-informed practice into a habit is experimenting with it in the classroom and seeing that it helps you meet your students' needs.

In particular, generic ideas about teaching (e.g. how to ask good questions or give good feedback) are generally insufficient at this stage. Teachers need expert support to turn generic ideas into specific ones for their context, e.g. 'how to ask good questions about triangles in Year 6' or 'how to give good feedback to Year 11 English students writing essays on King Lear'.

The best professional learning is rooted in both theory and practice – not just what is happening, but how and why.

For experts: make sure there is sufficient time to explore participants' existing ideas and assumptions, don't just impose your own advice immediately – especially for more experienced teachers. This avoids any sort of backfire effect where you accidentally strengthen existing views instead of overcoming them. Provide accessible summaries of evidence in teacher-friendly language. Be explicit about the weight of evidence and any opposing views. Encourage critical engagement with evidence. Don't focus only on research evidence and ignore practitioners and context.

For leaders/facilitators: ensure that participants have access to a good range of accessible expertise. Provide a culture in which ideas can be constructively questioned, including those from more senior leaders and teachers. This requires a supportive, trusting culture where professional learning is not linked to high-stakes judgements. Maintain a level of caution and scepticism to avoid overenthusiasm about novel ideas. Remember that your own perspective is inevitably more limited and biased than you'd want; show how you are open to new perspectives and ideas.

Do

- Do encourage and support practitioners to search for and find relevant research or evidence-informed strategies.
- Do engage with external expertise to help identify these and to help bring a different perspective.
- Do ensure that practitioners have support in taking generic advice and adapting it to their context.

Don't

- Don't expect everyone to know exactly where to go to for different evidence-informed strategies. It can take a lot of time for an individual teacher, and support from other colleagues or organisations is important.

■ Don't forget to critically evaluate the validity of different types of evidence before selecting your strategy.

Prepare, do and evaluate

Great professional learning includes *doing* and *evaluating*, not just listening or talking. The big question at all times is: 'Am I making an impact yet?'

The Responsive Professional Learning cycle requires that we:

1. **Prepare** what to do, how to do it, and how to know if it's having impact,
2. **Do** it in a real context, gather evidence of its impact and
3. **Evaluate** the evidence.

As we illustrated in the opening diagram, this phase is a mini cycle of its own.

Preparing

Trying out something new is challenging. Each interaction with a student or colleague leaves an impact; professional learning that is well prepared is more likely to have positive impact and well-prepared teachers are more likely to see success (Figure 3.3).

There are two elements to effective preparation:

■ Planning
■ Practising

Planning

As we discussed in Chapter One, our brains are constantly predicting what is about to happen and then comparing reality against that expectation. This feedback mechanism makes the learning faster and deeper. Our attention is engaged more strongly when something unexpected happens.

FIGURE 3.3   'By failing to prepare, you are preparing —to fail.' — *Benjamin Franklin*

Source: https://commons.wikimedia.org/wiki/File:Franklin-Benjamin-LOC-head.jpeg

In professional learning, participants need to focus their attention on the object of the learning, not get distracted by side issues.

To facilitate that process, it is helpful for participants to create a clear plan of what they expect to happen. This is a helpful collaborative exercise to sharpen up intentions and expectations. This clarity means that any gap between expectations and reality will be easier to identify. This prompts greater attention to the differences that matter, and also prompts curiosity as to why it did not go as planned.

One possible structure is to use the table below – which may in many instances develop into further rows:

I will ... (because...)	They will ... (because)	We will evaluate and collect evidence by...	What actually happened

In this first column, the participant identifies the actions that they will take. Optionally, they can make brief notes about the logic behind each step.

> **Example 1** *I will say 'I need you to form a straight, tidy line and stand in silence facing me'. I will make a gesture to show where the line will go. I will repeat the instruction. This should be a clear and easy instruction to understand, with the success criteria built in.*

> **Example 2** *I will start the meeting by saying 'thank you for meeting with me. I wanted to talk about a concern that I have. I'm going to say what I think has happened and then I'd like you to give me your perspective on it – I want to make sure that I haven't missed or misunderstood anything. Is that okay?' I'll do this to avoid fudging the start of the meeting with awkward small talk which often leads to me being unclear about the issue.*

In the next column, the participants identify how they think others would respond to this. If focusing on classroom practice, this would be a prediction of how students will react or behave. If working on leadership practice, this would be how a colleague would react or behave. Optionally, they briefly write the underlying assumptions that led to this prediction.

> **Example 1**: *Some of the students will follow the instruction quickly, others will hear me but assume that they can form the usual crowd by the door as that's what normally happens. Others may not even hear me but might start noticing others moving.*

> **Example 2**: *My colleague will probably go red and look uncomfortable but say 'yes, of course'.*

In the third column the participants record evaluation strategies that accompany this element. Some evaluation (e.g. videoing a lesson or meeting, or collecting exercise books at the end) may be a strategy for the whole lesson; not every line needs its own specific evaluation approach.

In the optional final column, the participant writes an observation of what actually happened. We'll explore this later.

This formal structure is very helpful but can also be quite time-consuming. If participants have a lot of experience, then it can be unhelpful to script familiar scenarios in detail; participants can just focus on key features. If the planning discussion is only shortly before the implementation, it could be a short verbal discussion, though details can easily get lost this way. On the other hand, novices may need to spend more time imagining and detailing what could happen.

An alternative approach is to take an existing lesson plan and annotate it with some additional detail about what is expected from students. Again, more experienced teachers may want to focus closely on a small element.

For experts: don't dominate the planning with your own thoughts – participants need to develop their own thinking to be ready to identify differences. Consider suggesting activities or approaches to gather evidence during implementation. Prompt participants to consider why they think that students may react in certain ways – what are the underlying assumptions?

For leaders/facilitators: provide a safe, trusting space for preparation and practice. Ensure that other workload doesn't impede participants' ability to prepare properly. You may need to challenge participants on the level of planning needed if you feel that they are thinking in insufficient or excessive detail.

Practising

There is significant value in rehearsing any techniques before they are used 'live'. For novice practitioners, this can reduce stress and help a practice flow more easily. For expert practitioners, it can be helpful to rehearse a familiar technique with a focus on what is different from normal habits – this reduces the chance of the practitioner reverting to habit under stress in the classroom.

Doug Lemov's *Teach Like a Champion*[3] techniques can be extremely useful here. They include clear step-by-step instructions and underlying rationale, and there are many exemplars of their being used successfully. (An important caveat is that these plausible techniques have not yet been researched at scale, despite their popularity.)

In our opinion, Lemov's techniques are likely to be best used within this Responsive Professional Learning cycle. Rather than starting with a technique to learn and then trying to parrot it, novice teachers can use the Teach Like a Champion book as a toolkit to solve problems that they've identified. The Responsive Professional Learning cycle ensures that they remain fully focused on student learning rather than getting overly obsessed with whether they appear to be repeating the steps correctly.

There are a number of caveats and cautions around practice:

1. Be very cautious about 'role-playing' scenarios. Even though some people enjoy these, many people find this activity painfully embarrassing and uncomfortable, while others throw themselves into it and do funny impressions. Both issues distract from effective learning.

2. It is easy to get over-focused on the performance, not the impact. A teacher can appear to be ticking all the boxes with a practice, such asking effective questions, but this is irrelevant if the only impact is making the lessons appear more pleasing or making lesson observers happier about what the teacher is doing. Worse still, where the focus is on repeating a technique accurately, it makes the teacher focused on their own performance and takes their attention away from impact on students.

Focus relentlessly on making practices work in context and evaluating how and why they have an impact on student learning.

3. There is a tension between *fidelity* and *adaptivity*. Fidelity is needed to ensure that teachers keep the 'active ingredients' of a practice – the elements that make it really effective. However, no two teachers are the same and no two classes are the same. Adaptivity enables the practice to be adapted to a teacher's own style and to the needs and context of each class. Too much focus on fidelity and a teacher loses their ability to respond and combine techniques, focusing on the technical process rather than meeting the needs of the organisational edge – the students, families and communities that they serve. Too much focus on adaptivity and teachers end up losing all the important features while mistakenly thinking that they've mastered the approach when all they've done is put a sticking plaster over existing practice.

For inexperienced teachers, this element of professional learning will need more modelling from expert practitioners, more chances to perform and get feedback from the expert, and more focus on breaking down each element to explain it. It is often helpful to focus on smaller segments of lessons rather than tackling large sequences of teaching all in one go.

For more experienced teachers, it may be more helpful to support them to contrast their own practice with another example, with the focus on impact rather than 'who is doing it better'. Effective learning may also require them to reflect more on why they currently practise the way they do – this helps make automatic habits more visible, clarifying underlying assumptions and making it easier to change practice in future. All of this requires a high level of trust and mutual respect.

For experts: provide clear models of practices or ideas to be tried, highlighting the most important elements with simple explanation of what makes them effective and why.

For leaders/facilitators: provide a safe, trusting space for preparation and practice. Ensure that other workload doesn't impede participants' ability to prepare properly.

Do

- Do be clear on what you expect to happen when you plan an approach, so that you can more clearly evaluate whether the impact matches your predictions.
- Do be aware of how much culture plays into this aspect of Responsive Professional Learning, if colleagues feel wary of experimenting or innovating, this will be difficult.

Don't

- Don't fall into the trap of unreliably evaluating performance. For example, judgemental lesson grades are inaccurate and tend to be focused on performance rather than impact on students' learning.
- Don't forget to sustain this over time so that it can be refined and embedded. A one-off exercise is unlikely to have much impact.

Doing and evaluating

There comes a moment in any professional learning when you have to put your ideas into action. The Responsive Professional Learning approach means there has been plenty of preparation, but, when it comes down to it, you've got to commit to giving it a go.

Try and arrange for preparation to be as close to the 'doing' as possible. Participants need to have the intentions fresh in their heads.

While implementing the practice or idea, there are some key elements to consider.

1. Fidelity: focus on the most important practices or changes so that they don't get lost.
2. Evaluation: constantly gather observations and evidence – is this really having impact? Much of the evaluation of any change in practice will occur during implementation – particularly those lessons that come from careful observation.
3. Wide-angle view: what else is happening? Is there anything else important that you might be missing?

This phase of the process is where participants fill in the fourth column in our suggested table:

I will ... (because ...)	They will ... (because ...)	We will evaluate and collect evidence by...	*What actually happened*

If in a classroom, focus mainly on what students do or say. If in a staff meeting, focus on what colleagues are seen to do or say. Try and avoid writing down inferences or guesses about how someone was thinking or feeling, or what you guess they have learned – these may well be your inferences rather than reality. Instead, focus on noting down relevant actions.

The implementation process should be kept separate from any high-stakes performance management or accountability processes. To be clear: there should be no requirement to use observations and evidence from this process for appraisal purposes (though some participants may later wish to volunteer it). The success of the implementation should not be tied to a performance management goal – it must be clear that the focus is on long-term learning not immediate success. There should be no attempt to measure the quality of teaching: no graded lesson observations.

For experts: be clear that you are focusing on gathering evidence of impact, not focusing on judging performance. Ensure that any other observers are not interrupting or disrupting the learning process. Look for subtle or unusual behaviours that less experienced observers might miss.

For leaders/facilitators: consider ways to flag that a classroom or meeting is in 'learning mode' to discourage interruptions. This could be a 'do not disturb, professional learning in progress' message on a door or it could be finding a location where it is harder to disturb the process. Also consider how you can make it clear that mistakes will be met with support and understanding: some schools keep a more senior leader or teacher nearby in case the professional learners need support.

Other forms of evaluation

Much of the evaluation should have taken place during the implementation – indeed, this will have built on evaluation that took place in the diagnostic phase. However, when an implementation activity has finished there may be follow-up evaluation to do. This could be, for example:

■ Carrying out a short interview or survey with certain students – you may wish to ask them to tell you about their general impressions or to explain their reflections on a specific activity.
■ Asking a colleague to email their reflections from a meeting.

- Collecting evidence from a task that is completed straight after the implementation, such as homework or a piece of work from the following lesson.
- Participants writing down their personal reflections from the process.

It's advisable to try and minimise the delay caused by follow-up evaluation. This ensures that the whole process is still fresh in participants' minds when they get to the reflection phase.

Reflect and sustain

This phase of the Responsive Professional Learning cycle is focused on:

1. Reflecting on what happened
2. Attempting to explain observations, drawing on the theory and evidence, to identify new learning and how to improve
3. Either:
   a. Reflecting back on the entire objective, checking newly discovered assumptions, identifying a better goal, exploring new evidence and expertise, *or*
   b. Trying out an improved approach with another cycle of prepare-do-evaluate, *or*
   c. Ensuring that the learning is embedded and shared.

Having implemented and evaluated an approach, the next step is to understand what happened. This normally takes place in a meeting after the implementation. Start the meeting by recapping the key aims identified: ideal outcomes, barriers, key evidence and chosen approach.

It is helpful to state key evidence observed or collected. This is best accomplished by simply presenting or summarising key observations, with a focus on whether it was expected, unexpected or whether there was something unanticipated that may be relevant.

To avoid the participant getting defensive or tense, it's important to focus on the impact that she or he had on students or colleagues. There should be no judgemental aspect on the teacher (positive or negative) and this should be delivered in a developmental culture where learning is celebrated. Useful example phrases are:

- 'We expected to see …. but instead we saw …'
- 'I also noticed that…'
- 'When you did [X], I heard the student say [Y]'

At this stage participants should avoid adding your interpretations or judgements until everyone has contributed their observations. Leave the '… because' or the '… was effective' until later.

Be aware of two issues:

- The temptation to focus on performance, not impact (e.g. 'you did that very well' or 'I think I used that correctly')
- The instinct to confuse collected evidence with inferences you have personally drawn about it (e.g. 'Jane looked scared' rather than 'Jane looked flushed and her speech was halting' or 'Mohammed learned that concept' rather than 'Mohammed wrote down correct answers to all three questions' – in both cases the latter observation is accurate where the former observation is an inference that may be incorrect)

If there is an expert present then it is helpful for them to leave their feedback until last, or even to prompt contributions about something specific – e.g. 'could you share what you observed about Peter when Mrs. Hill asked the class to start the test.'

In addition to stating observations from the process, it is helpful to share any other evidence collected. A facilitator, or a participant, should also re-state the logic behind collecting that piece of evidence, including what was expected or hoped for.

Once observations have been stated it is helpful to move on to discussing explanations. Give participants an opportunity to explore:

- How could we explain any discrepancies between expected and actual actions and outcome?
- What have we learned about how to remove the barriers?
- How far are we from our ideal outcome?
- Are we still asking the right question? Are there any other assumptions that we need to check?
- Is there anything else that we need to explore?
- What could we do better next time?

During this phase it can be helpful for an expert facilitator to bring some explanations, demonstrations and examples. It may help to split this discussion, identifying further reading or researching that is needed, then coming together again to reflect on this in light of the evidence from the professional learning. This could also be an excellent time to send one or more participants to a seminar or course to bring back further information, or to contact an external expert to share some findings and get support with interpretation and next steps.

Embedding learning

By this stage, staff have hopefully engaged with valuable new knowledge and may have overcome a common barrier to learning.

It is important to capture the learning in a way that will ensure that the practice is shared and sustained. To do this effectively, consider how you can ensure that better practice is sufficiently embedded in habits and resources so that all teachers can teach better without huge effort. It needs to be even easier to use the better approach than to use the old method. Too many good intentions get lost because we imagine that our future self has lots more time and energy than our current self! (See Figure 3.4.)

There's an analogy here with cooking. You can take lessons in being a better chef but still end up cooking very basic 'pasta and sauce' meals when you're busy, tired or stressed. To cook 'better by default' you need to make sure that you always have a stock of easy-to-use ingredients in the cupboard and that you have some easy-but-better dishes that can replace pasta.

In our experience, three of the most useful ways to sustainably embed learning are:

1. Update or refine assessments and tests for other teachers to use, with improved, simple guidance about how to interpret the findings.
2. Update and improve existing curriculum schemes and lesson plans in light of the new learning. This could include changing the sequence of lessons, embedding new activities and resources or annotating documentation with explanations and ideas from the professional learning.
3. Update policies, procedures and guidance to reflect new learning. This could include new guidance on how to conduct lessons, meetings or conversations or better ways to use systems. This is best accompanied by training sessions and Responsive Professional Learning cycles for other members of staff.

FIGURE 3.4   "The imaginary future-you problem."

It can also be helpful to record the learning that has taken place in other ways, such as:

- Writing up blogs and perhaps sharing via social media.
- Creating short video clips.
- Creating research posters to highlight key aims, ideas and outcomes.
- TeachMeet style presentations of three minutes each where a number of staff members share what they've been working on.
- Sharing notes or case studies through a structured shared online area.

It is important to consider the purpose of these and not to insist on burdensome tasks that might not be used well. However, in most cases we do find that colleagues are keen to share!

Structuring and implementing Responsive Professional Learning

Case study of responsive learning in classroom – Case Primary

A priority for Case Primary School is those children who are from disadvantaged family backgrounds. There is a large gap in terms of attainment between advantaged and disadvantaged children within the school. It is one of three key priorities across the school year.

One teacher at Case Primary School has about a third of his class that are from more economically disadvantaged families. Three boys within this group particularly concern him. They are disengaged and occasionally disruptive within class and their progress is also a concern. He asks a colleague to observe all three students and to look closely at their behaviour in lessons. He also compares the work they produce in different subjects and determines that writing is a key issue across the various subjects for all three. It is also observed that two of them produce little work but will ask questions around the topic area. The third child is frequently off-task and tends to disrupt the lesson by talking about irrelevant things.

The teacher works with a colleague to plan some strategies that research suggests should help disengaged boys. He tries them out in class, observed by the same colleague. They compare their work and behaviour to their notes from the previous observed lesson. Using these, they then adapt a couple of approaches and carry out another observed lesson. The teacher keeps reflective notes on what he notices in his other lessons and when marking work.

This is *Responsive* Professional Learning. It involves the key steps – identifying and diagnosing a need, selecting an evidence-informed strategy, and experimenting and evaluating that strategy until it best meets student needs. In the next section, we now explore some structured models of Responsive Professional Learning and explore how each has advantages and disadvantages.

Models of Responsive Professional Learning

Our Responsive Professional Learning cycle describes key features of effective professional learning. There are a number of formalised approaches to professional learning, aimed particularly at developing or changing adaptive classroom-based expertise. Here, we examine a few of the key features of a selection of these. Our aim is to illustrate how any one model is not perfect and how different features can make it more or less effective.

Lesson Study

Lesson Study is a process that has been used in Japan since the late 1800s. It has been much more widely adopted internationally since the late 1990s, with particularly notable uses in the USA, UK, Shanghai and Singapore.

Seleznyov (2017)[4] identifies seven key features:

1. *Identify focus*
   Compare long-term goals for student learning and development with their current characteristics in order to identify a school-wide research theme.
2. *Planning*
   Teachers work in collaborative groups to carry out *kyozai kenkyu* (study of material relevant to the research theme). This study leads to the production of a collaboratively written plan for a research lesson. This detailed plan attempts to anticipate pupil responses.
3. *Research lesson*
   The research lesson is taught by one teacher, who is a member of the collaborative planning group. Other members of the group act as silent observers, collecting evidence of pupil learning.
4. *Post-lesson discussion*
   The collaborative group meet to discuss the evidence they have gathered. Their learning in relation to the research theme is identified and recorded. It is intended that this learning feeds into subsequent cycles of research.
5. *Repeated cycles of research*
   Subsequent research lessons will be planned and taught that draw on the findings from the post-lesson discussions.
6. *Mobilising knowledge*
   Opportunities should be created for teachers working in one Lesson Study group to access and use the knowledge from other groups, either through observing other groups' research lessons or through the publication of group findings.

7. *Outside expertise*
   Where possible, there should be input from a *kochi* or 'outside expert' involved in the planning process and/or the research lesson.

We would also want to add that the *kochi* or 'knowledgeable other' should also be involved in the post-lesson discussion, both guiding discussion and providing an expert perspective on process and content.

In the UK, the model has seen widespread use, although the term has become extremely loosely defined, with many peer observation or co-planning processes now being labelled as 'Lesson Study' or 'lesson studies'. In particular, frequently missing features are:

- student learning focus: many UK implementations focus on teacher performance rather than student learning and its link to curriculum and assessment;
- co-planning: we frequently come across models where teachers jump straight to observing each other without carefully planning what they intend and anticipate;
- repeated cycles: many settings will use a single cycle rather than multiple repetitions and iterations;
- outside expertise: a number of schools engage in Lesson Study without external expertise (sometimes known as the *knowledgeable other*), without skilled facilitation and without structured engagement with research and evidence-informed assessment tools.

There is also a debate going on as to how faithful UK implementations of Lesson Study should be to those used in Japan. However, given the very different contexts and cultures, we would advise significant caution. In particular, teachers in England are held to account in a very different way to those in Japan, with a much more loosely defined and rapidly changing system of curriculum and assessment than Japan. Additionally, in Japan, teachers are able to explore a reasonably settled way to teach and assess a topic and refine in more depth, over time, with less immediate demand for impact and wider application.

To make Lesson Study work effectively, we recommend that the school should train internal champions or experts in the process, working with an expert external body. We tend to see more success where schools pilot the process with a few small groups before rolling it out more widely. It can also often helpful for all groups to pick from a few common key themes which align to school development plans. This also allows the school to commission higher quality external expert input for each theme.

Teacher Learning Communities

Professor Dylan Wiliam has developed a model of Responsive Professional Learning called TLCs or Teacher Learning Communities.[5] He wisely cautions that schools should first identify the content that should be learned before selecting a professional learning mechanism. However, for improving Assessment for Learning (AfL), he advocates the TLC model, supported by the following organisational supports:

- Choice: Wiliam suggests that teachers are best-placed to identify what to develop to support their students, as they best know their own strengths as well as those of their students.
- Flexibility: teachers should be able to pick, from a recommended menu, whichever AfL strategy they feel most comfortable with, while taking care to implement them with fidelity.

- Small steps: teachers should identify small aspects of their practice and make small changes – Wiliam argues that this is more likely to be sustainable than attempting large changes.
- Accountability: teachers should be held accountable to make improvements – not with high-stakes incentives but with an expectation that should be able to clearly articulate what they are trying to improve, why they are improving it and how they are doing so.
- Support: teachers should have access to expertise and facilitation to enable them to successfully pursue the change to which they are being held accountable.

Once these elements are in place, Wiliam suggests the following structures:

- Groups of ten to twelve teachers meeting for at least seventy-five minutes, once a month.
- In the first instance, teachers can be from different phases, year groups and subject areas, but in later years it can be useful to move into more similar age- or subject-focused groups.
- Meetings should be structured as:
  - Five minutes: introduction and present the agenda.
  - Five minutes: participants engage in a starter activity to focus on their learning.
  - Twenty-five minutes: participants feedback on what they had previously committed to do while others listen actively and appreciatively.
  - Twenty-five minutes: new learning about assessment is presented, through e.g. a video, a paper, a book or a speaker.
  - Fifteen minutes: action-planning is undertaken by each group member, setting times for any peer observation, identifying when they will try out ideas.
  - Five minutes: summarise learning from the session.

Wiliam notes that schools are always very tempted to vary this model or appropriate it to focus on other areas than Assessment for Learning, and cautions against this.

In our view, this model (as set out here) may not stress some key features of our RPL cycle. If using this model, we would suggest that:

- Teachers may need more support to translate generic Assessment for Learning ideas into their own subject areas and specific topics to be taught. This needs to link to thinking about how subjects are best taught, sequenced and assessed.
- Teachers may need support to identify intended student impact, seek out the best possible pedagogical evidence and reveal their own inbuilt assumptions.
- It could well be that teachers identify barriers to student learning which are not related to AfL ideas, so it seems reasonable to allow teachers to explore outside this area as long as they continue to search for high-impact approaches.

We would also note that, while Wiliam suggests that teacher choice is helpful, the *Developing Great Teaching* review of evidence notes that professional learning can also be successful where teachers are 'conscripted' into the process – but only if the teachers do become genuinely persuaded of the value of what they are doing. Our experience also suggests that, where all teachers exercise totally free choice in their Lesson Study, there can be a lack of coherence across the school's programme of professional learning and a lack of sustainability of any one focus.

Spirals of Enquiry

The Spirals of Enquiry model originates from British Columbia, Canada, designed by Halbert and Kaser (Figure 3.5).[6]

This model has a number of similarities to the Responsive Professional Learning cycle. Where it varies from our RPL cycle is that it explicitly starts with exploring students' own experience of learning whereas our cycle draws from a broader possible range of perspectives on student learning. Halbert and Kaser suggest that, by forcing teachers to begin with students' perspectives, they are able to stop teachers from always thinking about performance and techniques and to give them fresh perspectives on what it is like to be a learner in their classrooms.

It may well be that there are occasions where forcing teachers to consider only the students' perspective may be helpful. This could be helpful in a school where the focus for many years has been on teacher appraisal, teacher performance and high-stakes evaluation. In this sort of context, teachers can often obsess about how they are judged to be performing, even where a process is explicitly focused on student learning.

However, we would also caution that, while students' perspectives are important, they can rarely, for example, give entirely new insights into what is possible where the majority of students have only ever experienced one type of teaching or one type of school. It can be important to see how students learn in other schools, and also to get experienced expert practitioners' perspectives on what is happening.

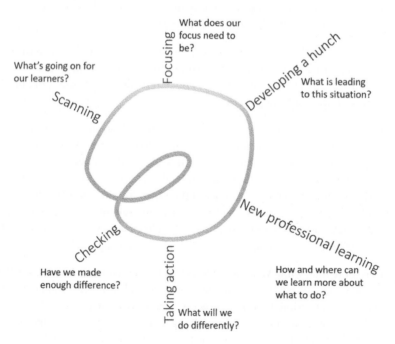

FIGURE 3.5 The Spirals of Enquiry model of Halbert and Kaser.

Professional Learning Communities

'PLCs' is another term, such as Lesson Study and TLCs, which has become a catch-all for groups of teachers learning together. However, one particular model of PLC is the one defined by DuFour, Eaker and DuFour[7] which has three 'big ideas':

1. Ensure that students learn
   a. Start with three key questions
      i.   What do we want each student to learn?
      ii. How will we know when the student has learned it?
      iii. How will we respond when a student experiences difficulty in learning it?
   b. Respond rapidly to difficulty:
      i.   *Timely.* The school quickly identifies students who need additional time and support.
      ii. Based on *intervention* rather than *remediation*. The plan provides students with help as soon as they experience difficulty rather than relying on summer school, retention, and remedial courses.
      iii. *Directive.* Instead of inviting students to seek additional help, the systematic plan requires students to devote extra time and receive additional assistance until they have mastered the necessary concepts.
2. A culture of collaboration
   a. Teachers work in teams, engaging in ongoing cycles of questions and inquiry that promote team learning. Collaboration must be more than mere congeniality and consensus.
   b. Schools must make sure that everyone belongs to a team that has time to meet during the work day, throughout the year.
   c. Teams must focus their efforts on crucial questions related to learning and generate products that reflect that focus, such as lists of essential outcomes, different kinds of assessment, analyses of student achievement and strategies for improving results.
   d. Teams must develop norms or protocols to clarify expectations regarding roles, responsibilities and relationships among team members.
   e. Teams must adopt student achievement goals linked with school and district goals.
3. A focus on results
   a. Teachers must embrace data as a useful indicator of progress
   b. Participants must stop disregarding unfavourable data and stop making excuses
   c. Participants must commit to using collective effort to solve problems and achieve results, not work in isolation.

These ideas come from a US context where teachers are often particularly isolated due to lack of shared curriculum and assessments. As a possible caveat, it is strongly focused on collecting and analysing test data which could well miss other key evaluation approaches, and assumes that existing tests are valid and sufficiently focused on key learning. There is also a lack of emphasis, in our view, of external expert input, leaving teachers relying on whatever they currently know in order to solve the problems that they are experiencing.

If adopting a 'PLC' approach then we would suggest that participants cast the net wider than merely analysing data, and that the school commissions external experts to help with both facilitation and also the curriculum, assessment and pedagogical content being explored.

Adapting the Responsive Professional Learning cycle

The RPL cycle is ideal for professional learning aimed at developing classroom-based adaptive expertise or for staffroom-based deliberative expertise.

However, it is a flexible model that can be adapted to some other contexts. We describe below how we have seen the RPL cycle effectively adapted.

Starting with observation

If you have opportunities for lesson observations and wish to build these into an RPL cycle, you could use them for:

a. Initial diagnostic work: use the observer to identify possible barriers to student learning as a starting point to the RPL cycle; or
b. Observation of student learning in the implementation phase: gathering data from the classroom about how students are reacting to new strategies being trialled.

If using option (b), the observer can meet with the teacher before the observation to ask:

i. What is it that you are teaching, where does it fit in the curriculum, how do the activities lead to greater understanding or remove barriers, and how are you assessing learning?
ii. How have you chosen your teaching strategies? What is your evidence that they are likely to be effective? Where have you looked for evidence?
iii. What would success look like? Which students should I observe in particular and which data should I collect to help you determine if it has been a success?

Our advice would be that a developmental cycle of Responsive Professional Learning shouldn't also be used for appraisal purposes – we explore this in more detail in Chapter Four.

We would also strongly suggest that observations of *teacher* performance are not used as the starting point for Responsive Professional Learning. For example, 'I think your lesson was not satisfactory' or 'you need to improve your differentiation' are almost certain to make professional learners focus on their own performance rather than student learning. In both cases, it would be far more helpful to identify an initial hunch about an issue with student learning then work with the teacher to test those assumptions before identifying a teacher action or intervention.

Starting with research, teaching approach or an expert engagement

We frequently speak to senior leaders who are keen for their teachers to engage with a specific piece of research or theory, or who would like certain teachers to work on certain aspects of their teaching practice.

Our caution is that this is potentially putting the cart before the horse – giving someone an answer to try before they know what the question is.

But there will occasionally be good reasons to start this way and if you are starting with a piece of research or expertise:

■ Examine which assumptions lead you to think that this may be helpful, so that you can test these;

■ Identify what the research tells you about possible barriers to students' learning; then

■ Go back to a diagnostic phase to identify whether these barriers exist in your class-room *and* whether they are the most pressing ones.

■ Finally, if those barriers are present and still a priority, use the research to identify which practices to implement and evaluate in the classroom.

If you are starting with a specific teacher practice:

■ Examine which assumptions lead you to think that this particular practice is a prior-ity for these teachers;

■ Identify what challenges and barriers you might see in specific lessons if these prac-tices are not being used effectively; then

■ Go back to a diagnostic phase to identify whether these barriers exist in your class-room *and* whether they are the most pressing ones.

■ Finally, if those barriers are present and still a priority, use research and expert guid-ance about the practice to identify which practices to implement and evaluate in the classroom.

Example 1

Mr Jones has recently read some blogs about cognitive learning science and memory and is keen to share these with his colleagues. He identifies that a key challenge that this area of practice can overcome is the issue of students forgetting key ideas or being poor at revision for examinations. He asks each subject department in his school to meet and discuss where they see the biggest issues with forgetting. He organises a training session to which subject leaders are asked to bring the results of these discus-sions, where he invites an expert in memory, cognitive science and teaching. Teachers have now identified key barriers for specific students and the expert can work with them to explore the theory behind this and help the design ways to address this in their lessons.

Following the input, teachers work back in subject teams to try out ideas to improve memorisation, including the use of spaced learning and interleaving. Over the course of the next six months they meet regularly to explore the evidence about impact and which additional barriers they need to overcome. Mr Jones keeps tabs on each department's pro-gress, sharing ideas where necessary. He asks the memory expert back after four months to provide support, challenge and new ideas.

This example is likely to have more impact than merely presenting ideas on memory and asking teachers to apply them. However, the missing element here is Mr Jones checking his assumptions about whether the issue of forgetting is really the most pressing issue in the school. Perhaps his own biases caused by his own enthusiasm for the idea mean that he is missing bigger issues which other staff can help him find?

Example 2

Ms Smith is worried that some children in her school are being too passive in lessons. She wants to stop teachers only asking for contributions from those with hands up and decides to use the Teach Like a Champion 'Cold Call' approach. She asks each class teacher to identify three students who rarely put their hands up and conduct a short interview with each to ask them about their experience in class. The teachers bring their findings to a workshop where they share and discuss them and then watch some videos on the 'cold call' technique.

Following the workshop, teachers try to implement the technique in at least three lessons, with some of them volunteering to record video clips while others invite colleagues in to their lessons to observe the impact. In a follow-up workshop, the teachers share and explore what has been working and what has been less successful.

This example appears to be better than simply presenting ideas on 'cold call' and asking teachers to use them. However, there are a number of elements missing here. Firstly, Ms Smith doesn't conduct a diagnostic phase. Because she has already determined her chosen solution, she leaves no room for the exploration of the problem to highlight other, more pressing interventions. For example, perhaps some of the students who don't contribute have issues with language, or are missing some prior knowledge to enable them to participate fully? It would have been better if she had used the teachers' exploration interviews with the reticent students as a starting point to search for underlying issues. It may well be that some of the teachers eventually chose to use a 'cold call' technique but it may also be that a more open process could have elicited deeper understanding of issues and gained greater buy-in from teachers.

Practical guide to implementing models of Responsive Professional Learning

RPL can be adapted to different contexts but it can also be hard to structure and implement. Below is some guidance to help you consider how you might implement the RPL cycle in practice.

How do you find time for Responsive Professional Learning?

Responsive Professional Learning should be sustained over time with iterative opportunities for expert input, experimentation in the classroom, evaluation and collaboration. Later in the book we explore in more detail how to structure and enable time for professional learning but here are some possible tips:

1. *Use of video to enable peer observation.* This can certainly help with timetabling and enabling collaboration, although it can't necessarily allow participants to focus on the relevant places and moments in a lesson. Video could allow participants to collaborate remotely, saving travel time, though there is always a time cost involved - someone has to sit down and watch the video at some point and potentially decide which clips to use and share.
2. *Meeting time.* Review how many team or whole school meetings could be replaced by better email communication, so that you can maximise teachers' time to be focused on teaching, learning and development and move administrative and briefing tasks into electronic communication.

3. *Covering lessons.* Many schools invest in staff to allow teachers to more flexibly request someone to take their normal lesson. This can free them up to observe another colleague. Some schools give each teacher a fixed allocation of professional learning cover that they can use each year – subject to availability of staff.

4. *Focus on parts of lessons, rather than whole lessons.* This involves freeing up teachers to watch ten to fifteen segments of lessons rather than full lessons. Many schools find this easier to resource and it also reduces the amount of meeting time needed to plan before-hand and for discussion afterwards. Depending on the area of focus, this may not be appropriate, but encouraging regular peer observation and collaboration, even for short periods of time helps build in iterative, cyclical opportunities to develop as well as building it into a normal part of how we work, supporting the development of the right culture and norms.

How can you encourage and support effective collaboration?

Unfocused collaboration, where teachers share or discuss ideas with no clear purpose or intended action, is unlikely to have an impact on practice and students. Yet, even without impact, these activities are often valued by staff.

In some schools we have worked with, we have suggested that introducing some initially superficial discussion of ideas may be a helpful first step in establishing a new culture of sharing. One school introduced a 'bring and brag' weekly segment in the whole school staff meeting, where one teacher each week was asked to share one idea they'd recently tried. This turned out to be a valuable first step in a school where there was previously no history of collaboration, where pedagogy was rarely discussed. However, senior leaders were extremely clear that this was simply the first step of many in transforming the approach to professional learning – they were clear on the shortcomings of the approach.

All schools should be working towards more focused collaboration, which involves an element of challenge and is focused on evaluating the impact of practice on students. Below are some tips for building this:

1. Good leaders provide good role models. Leaders should model their own professional learning and how they are open to innovating and critically evaluating the impact of their practice. Professional learning can be a very vulnerable process in many ways, so leaders actively modelling and demonstrating this contributes significantly to a safe culture where others feel safe to do the same. In one school, the headteacher used videos of his own lessons and invited critique, showing how each week he took on new ideas and built them in. This helped to overcome a previously top-down culture and showed that everyone in the school could be a learner.

2. Demonstrate what a really good professional learning focus question looks like. There is a temptation to choose something that is too large or to aim to change too many things at once, as we are all motivated to meet the many and complex needs of our students. However, too broad a question (such as 'how can I develop the literacy of my students?' or 'what are the best ways for increasing engagement in my classroom?') will involve many different strategies and factors. It will also be difficult to be responsive to the varied and many needs of students within such a theme, and the measures needed to judge success will be so varied that it becomes impractical. Discussing a clearer question, of the form 'what is the impact of [evidence-informed

strategy] on [particular learning need] for [particular group of students]?' will allow much more effective Responsive Professional Learning.

3. Using mentors and facilitators in the organisation. It can be helpful to develop certain practitioners to be experts in the Responsive Professional Learning process, or parts of the professional learning process. For example, helping practitioners to find research and evidence-informed strategies, helping practitioners to focus their learning and develop an enquiry questions, helping practitioners to evaluate and identify what good success criteria would be. However, often facilitators in schools do not have the time and support to develop themselves and their own practice. Be aware of making sure that all your staff are engaged in developing their own practice and meeting their students' needs.

4. Be flexible around collaboration. The research shows us that it doesn't matter whether teachers are initially conscripts or volunteers in their professional learning process as long as they eventually genuinely believe in the value of the process. This would suggest that you can allocate who collaborates with who. However, it is worth being aware of the powerful cultural contribution of staff having some control over the way they collaborate. Most importantly, colleagues should collaborate around a topic that they all believe is important.

How do you support engagement with external expertise?

Getting teachers to engage with external experts often involves a significant amount of money and time. Some ways to address this are:

1. Use internal expertise. Where different subjects have particular expertise (e.g. English teachers may be able to support other subjects in building longer written responses), colleagues may be able to offer expertise and evidence-informed strategies. Be wary of just sharing ideas, however. Time is needed to take new ideas and refine and embed them in the classroom through Responsive Professional Learning processes.

2. Engage with research, blogs, research-informed summaries, etc.

3. When you do invest in an external expert, ensure that the investment is worthwhile by supporting practitioners with the time and support to refine and embed their new learning through Responsive Professional Learning.

What type of evidence might practitioners be evaluating in their Responsive Professional Learning?

If we follow Daniel Willingham and define learning as something that has been committed to long-term memory, then it is extremely hard to measure it in the short-term. As we explored in Chapter Two, building long term memory occurs through repeated recall, over time. This makes it very difficult to immediately evaluate the success of a teacher and the impact of their practice. As Professor Rob Coe says[8], the following are poor proxies for learning – they are commonly used but don't really tell us a great deal about what has been learned nor do they correlate particularly with the amount of learning that has taken place:

- Students are busy: lots of work is done (especially written work).
- Students are engaged, interested and motivated.
- Classroom is ordered, calm and under control.

- Curriculum has been covered (i.e. presented to students in some form).
- (At least some) students have supplied correct answers, even if they
  - have not really understood them;
  - could not reproduce them independently;
  - will have forgotten them by next lesson; and/or
  - already knew how to do this anyway.

However, there are ways to get some sense of learning environment. For example, if misbehaviour is a barrier to learning, then exploring how to reduce that we can reasonably assume will help reduce a barrier to effective learning.

Here are some options to evaluate to inform Responsive Professional Learning.

Issues around behaviour or disengagement in lessons, which are barriers to learning

- Quality of work produced.
- Number of times on/off task.
- Number of times contributed to lesson vocally.
- Amount of time taken to start work.
- Nature of conversations with peers (e.g. around work, etc.).

Issues around memory and retaining ideas

- Looking at work over time – is there evidence of a skill developing, of knowledge being retained, of misconceptions reducing and not reappearing?
- In a lesson that includes repetition from a previous one, observing how long it takes students to remember and apply previous learning (if at all).
- In a lesson that includes repetition from a previous one, observing the questions asked by students or perhaps the conversations they have with each other as they remember or recap this understanding.
- In a lesson that includes repetition from a previous one, observing carefully the misconceptions that arise or whether they arise.

Issues around a particular topic or area

- Specific analysis of work (e.g. number of times certain vocabulary used, number of times certain tenses used, number of times misconception in Maths applied, number of longer questions correctly answered, etc.). Broader outcomes or focuses are harder to respond to or account for.
- Observation of how student approaches topic (e.g. amount of time on/off task, which stage takes longest, discussions between students, etc.).
- Comparisons to previous equivalent groups, comparisons to similar subject areas.
- A pre- and post- test or baseline.

An important caveat for all of these is that one or several of these indicators may appear to be getting more positive over time without any real improvement in learning, particularly the first section around engagement.

Finally, we'd advise having individual or small group conversations with students about their own work, their attitudes to learning and their wider goals and feelings. Surveys can also be useful, albeit with less opportunity to follow particular avenues of inquiry.

Evaluation of a professional learning programme

In this section, we look at how a leader might evaluate a whole programme of professional learning and the activities within it. We'll review the different levels of impact achieved through professional learning and how these could be assessed.

This section might also be helpful to providers or leaders of professional learning as we explore the principles of evaluating a professional learning programme more broadly.

Micro versus macro evaluation

It is possible to evaluate small, rapid changes or large ones that take a long time. Continually evaluating small – *micro* – changes gives you rapid feedback about the impact of a specific intervention so that you can keep adapting what you are doing.

Examples of micro evaluation could include:

- Question-by-question analysis of an end of topic test to explore patterns of understanding in different areas of the topic.
- Capturing a ten-minute clip showing how a teacher introduced a practical task and what happened next with specific students.
- A short observation of a line management meeting in which the manager is trying to adopt more of a coaching style.

However, sometimes we also need to look at large changes and impacts. Macro evaluation explores the overall effect of hundreds of complex changes and effects. It is typically exploring impact over a longer period of time over a larger number of people. It's harder to identify which individual process or individual caused the changed but it's a helpful look back, answering the question: 'how did we do overall'?

Examples of macro evaluation – i.e. looking at longer-term impacts, perhaps aggregated from many smaller changes – that we've seen schools use have included:

- Asking a whole class to complete a past exam paper and seeing, on average, how their grades compare to previous attempts;
- Multiple ratings of a teacher's classroom performance using a generic set of descriptors of what 'outstanding practice' looks like; and
- A questionnaire for participants to give their overall impressions of a whole day of training.

These macro evaluations are generally much less helpful in Responsive Professional Learning. There could be hundreds of factors that impact these overall results. It's nigh on impossible to try and identify the impact of one small programme of professional learning on overall test scores for a whole subject. If teachers are under pressure to prove such a link then they will almost certainly prioritise training students to score well on exams rather than focusing on the underlying quality of learning. Similarly, if a professional learning programme is supposed to show an overall impact on 'quality of teaching' then participants and facilitators will be incentivised to focus on producing a better-looking performance in front of an observer – something that has been shown to have little correlation with better quality student learning.

Nevertheless, there is a place for some macro evaluation. Ultimately, we do want small micro effects to cumulatively create a macro impact. It is reasonable to explore whether a package of different professional learning programmes are gradually having an impact on overall grades, or on teachers' overall confidence, for example.

There is a continuum from micro to macro, this is not a binary categorisation. In Responsive Professional Learning, as described earlier in this chapter, we focus mainly on micro evaluation. A key part of a senior leaders' roles is to enable, promote and encourage Responsive Professional Learning.

However, a school leader may also need to take steps to try and evaluate the overall impact of individual professional learning programmes or even the entire professional learning approach. This can help the school to evaluate, for example:

- whether a programme appears to have achieved its overall goals;
- whether, in view of the cost and time taken, it has achieved value for money and value for time; and
- what other learning needs have been identified and highlighted through the programme.

Evaluating a specific programme of professional learning

To evaluate a programme of professional learning it is useful to consider the nature of the planned impact (direct or indirect) and its depth (adaptive, deliberative, procedural or awareness). See Chapter Two for a more detailed exploration of these levels.

1. Direct impact

   This refers to any professional learning that is targeted at specific benefits for students, families and community that the school serves, i.e. at the organisational edge. For example, you might be focused on developing oracy (spoken language skills), or improving the way that students understand and use algebraic graphs.

   At a micro level, staff might test student achievement in an assessment of their knowledge of simultaneous equations, or they might observe how often a child raises their hand to contribute in a particular lesson, or perhaps measure how often a child uses technical vocabulary. At a macro level, staff members might use standardised assessments to measure students' overall reading ages over time, compare overall performance in exams against target grades, or observe overall attendance or behaviour trends.

2. Indirect impact

   This refers to any professional learning aimed at improving the individual's, team's or organisation's ability to run smoothly and support staff. This includes leadership and management activities. Evaluation of impact could include:

   - Looking for evidence of changes in practice through observation of processes and meetings or monitoring activity records of processes.
   - Recording changes in systems and policies.
   - Collecting survey data or conducting interviews about perceptions of the change.
   - Formal assessments of staff members' skills and knowledge – e.g. a school leadership qualification.

Case study – evaluating safeguarding training

At Eagle High School, all new staff received training in safeguarding students. At the beginning of the session, to assess their awareness and understanding of the issue, staff were given a multiple-choice exercise where they had to select what they would do in the face of certain safeguarding challenges. They then received training from a Safeguarding Officer. At the end of the session, they completed the same multiple-choice exercise again. This evaluated their initial new understandings. After six weeks, a random selection of five of the staff were asked to repeat the same multiple-choice exercise to see if this knowledge had been retained. As they all answered appropriately, no further action was needed.

This is an example of procedural and deliberative expertise. The intention was to change participants' understanding of safeguarding and, when necessary, ensure the use of their new knowledge around safeguarding. The evaluation process was designed to measure whether participants had learned what they needed to, whether they knew how to deploy it when necessary, and whether they had retained this knowledge.

Case study – evaluating a school visit to get awareness of ideas to support high-attaining students

At Park Primary School, students with lower prior attainment tended to succeed very well, but the high prior attaining students tended to hit a plateau in their performance. It was a common picture across the school for many subject areas. It was likely that this was going to need to be a priority area for the school.

The school leadership decided that they needed to visit some other schools who were successfully stretching their higher attaining students. A number of schools were identified who had otherwise similar characteristics, and two middle leaders, the Headteacher and a classroom teacher visited three different schools. They identified a range of different techniques and spoke to colleagues from the school.

Following this process, different teams spent time observing their high prior attaining students and identified some trends. Using this as a basis for their diagnosis, alongside discussions and team meetings, they then selected two key approaches that they had seen at other schools that best seemed to fit their own students and their needs.

The act of visiting another school is a fairly short-term engagement in professional learning. The members of staff are being externally facing and using other schools' experiences to inform their decision making. They will evaluate the strategies they choose quite carefully, but the act of visiting another school builds awareness and does not need to be evaluated beyond 'did we find something useful that we took forward?'. It is not reasonable to expect a change in practice after short-term engagement with another school. It is the processes that follow that that need to be evaluated in full.

Guskey's levels

A professional learning process is often meeting a number of different needs, some of which are easier to identify and evaluate than others. When speaking to teachers, it often takes some thought to consider what specific student need they are trying to address. For example, try asking a teacher what specific benefit they want for their students if they improve their feedback. What would it really look like? It's hard to do!

To help with this, Thomas Guskey's *Evaluating Professional Development* breaks down evaluation of professional learning to five different levels[9] which can help structure your thinking. Guskey's levels can also be used to help evaluate a whole-school programme of professional learning.

Participants' reaction

This tells you how colleagues initially respond to a professional learning activity. It might include whether the content felt relevant, whether the delivery was effective or just whether they enjoyed the experience. This is often collected through surveys at the end of sessions or interviews and focus groups. Tools such as Google surveys and various school improvement online tools can support this.

Participants' learning

This tells you whether colleagues have learnt any new knowledge or understanding and what that new knowledge or understanding is. This might be something that colleagues reflect on themselves, share with each other, or perhaps write up and record. Line management or team meetings might be a vehicle to support this, and learning may also be demonstrated through reflective journals, formal accreditations or self-audits of knowledge.

Organisation and support

This level examines the impact on the organisation and whether the organisation supported the implementation of any new learning. Was the organisational support there? Were there enough resources or was there enough time? This might be apparent through staff feedback (surveys or focus groups), in meetings or through school plans. Tools such as the Teacher Development Trust CPD Audit[10] looks at organisational support for effective professional learning in schools. This includes:

- Organisational culture
- Focus of professional learning programmes
- Evaluation approaches and tools used
- Career development opportunities
- Time and resource
- Engagement with evidence, research and higher education.

Participants' use of new knowledge and skills

Are teachers then *using* any new knowledge or understanding they have learnt? This tells you how well implemented the professional learning has been. It might be evident in lesson observations or feedback from staff through surveys or conversations. Low-stakes learning walks, line management meetings, peer observations (such as those within Lesson Study), can all support this and online performance management tools can also include self-evaluation tools to help teachers reflect on this.

Student learning outcomes

Finally, has there been an impact on students? This could be any outcome – attainment, behavioural or attitudinal, depending on what need your professional learning was planned to address. This could be measured using attainment data, student work, homework, questionnaires, observation or video. The responsive learning cycle focuses on supporting teachers to be evaluative practitioners, generating their own evidence as they engage.

These five levels can help you break down what need you are addressing and what impact you are evaluating. Guskey also points out that all levels are important and should be considered. Many school leaders would rightly prioritise student learning outcomes, and some school leaders might need to redress the balance between professional learning focused only on teacher learning and professional learning focused on students. Yet to address student learning outcomes, all the other levels need to be being met. If teachers haven't learnt anything new or changed their practice, impact on student outcomes is very unlikely.

Recently there has been a big move to dismiss 'happy sheets' that only inform you of participants' reactions. If you do not consider the delivery of professional learning, or how it is received, if it goes badly then the impact will be significantly reduced. Similarly, a school that has been through challenging changes in a short period of time may have jaded staff who are lacking in motivation after a gruelling time. Investing in an inspiring speaker who can re-engage staff to invest in their development and teaching, can have real dividends when followed up well. Teacher and staff satisfaction is important in its own right. As an organisation, it is also important to develop staff for their own sake to a certain extent, supporting retention, wellbeing, etc.

We would argue that, in many schools, not enough professional learning is linked to student outcomes, or specific student outcomes, but that does not mean we should throw the baby out with the bathwater and lose sight of these other levels.

In addition, Guskey also points out that all five levels depend on one another and build on the level before. Well delivered information helps change staff learning, with sufficient organisational support (e.g. time and resources), staff can then change their practice, and, finally, this change in practice can impact on students. This is another key reason why each level should be considered and planned for. Finally, these levels of evaluation are useful not only for planning evaluation, but also for planning your professional learning. (See our section on evaluation and diagnosis).

When considering your professional learning plan, where you are trying to develop adaptive skills (teaching and leadership), consider Guskey's levels and the theory of change that they outline. This can help you break down and clarify the different aspects of evaluation that you might consider.

To what extent does evaluation of professional learning constitute research?

A recent positive change within the education sector, and the wider world, is an increased awareness of research and research methodologies. Teachers and school leaders are increasingly aware of how different approaches to evaluation can help researchers to overcome their own biases, produce deeper insights, overcome confounding issues and result in more generalizable results.

There are differing views about how to go about evaluation in a school setting: to what extent should we be applying research methods and attempting to get generalizable results?

In our view, there are some principles that should be applied:

- High-quality assessment: wherever possible, include some nationally standardised assessments and work with assessment experts when designing tests. A good exploration and research phase of Responsive Professional Learning may highlight some high-quality, validated assessment tools to use.
- Pre and post testing: always try and engage in diagnostic assessment before engaging in an intervention, in order to identify what change has been made.
- Collecting data and artefacts: try and gather video or audio clips, work samples, test papers, interview transcripts, etc. so that they can be later analysed by

others. This is superior to simply relying on staff members' own recollections and interpretations.

There are other principles which may not always be appropriate:

- Control group: it can sometimes be helpful to identify two similar groups and then try an intervention on one group, in order to compare the effects of the intervention versus what would have happened anyway. In our view, this can be helpful to highlight differences but at the level of small groups of students or even two classes, there are likely to be so many hidden differences between the two groups that it is unlikely to make any final result more valid nor generalisable.
- Randomisation: An extension of the above principle is randomisation, where researchers across a large population (e.g. 500 students or more) randomly assign students to one of two groups. Laws of probability suggest that both groups are likely to be fairly similar – this is more likely to be the case the higher the number of students. Most schools will find this extremely difficult to do and any final experimental results are still likely to be limited as they can only tell you about the specific population from which the samples are drawn – e.g. something about students in your school rather than about all students across the world. There is little practical benefit in randomising smaller numbers of students (e.g. ten to fifteen in each group) as the likelihood of significant differences across the two groups remains very high. Additionally, drawing reasonably sized, properly random samples from a school population will still only tell you something probably about that school population – it can't tell you about the wider student population across the country or the world as the school's community hasn't been randomly selected from this wider population.

The aim of evaluation within school-based professional learning is to help to focus practitioners on specific details of what is happening, while attempting to increase clarity of intent and reduce bias about results. The mere of act of attempting to evaluate your practice would appear to make it more likely that a positive impact is seen in students. It is typically not able to produce generalisable results given the scale and methodology used.

Ultimately, we are looking for professional learning to have evaluation that is *internally valid* – i.e. describing the true state of affairs within a class or school, rather than *externally valid* – i.e. describing the true state of affairs outside of the setting in which it is conducted. Similarly, evaluation within professional learning is typically focused on the how and the why, rather than identifying or quantifying a provable impact.

When presenting results from Responsive Professional Learning, it is helpful to detail:

- Information about your school and wider context;
- Which processes you used to assess and evaluate; and
- Which sources of evidence and research you used, and why, including which experts you engaged with.

If you feel that you may have discovered a more generalisable finding, then we would recommend contacting a higher education institution in order to plan a more formal experiment where the approach can be tested at larger scale in order to confirm this.

Checklists

Checklist for a senior leader of professional learning

- ☐ Are staff engaged in evaluative processes and Responsive Professional Learning? Is this at the heart of our professional learning process?
- ☐ What is the balance between direct and indirect impact in our professional learning programme?
- ☐ What is the balance between staff engaging in building awareness, procedural, deliberative or adaptive expertise?
- ☐ How do we evaluate our professional learning programme at each of Guskey's levels?

Checklist for starting the leadership of a professional learning process

- ☐ What is the need that I am seeking to address?
- ☐ What would it look like if I was successful?
- ☐ Do I expect to impact on student outcomes?
- ☐ If so, how am I supporting staff to enable Responsive Professional Learning and evaluate their own learning?
- ☐ How will I collate this evaluation and learning?
- ☐ How will I know if staff are enabled to change their practice?
- ☐ How will I know if staff's understanding has changed?

Checklist for a middle leader

- ☐ Does my team engage in Responsive Professional Learning and is this shared amongst colleagues?
- ☐ Can my team talk about specific students they hope to support?
- ☐ Can they describe what it would look like if they were successful?
- ☐ Is the balance right between developing awareness, procedural, deliberative or adaptive expertise among the team?

Checklist for a classroom teacher

- ☐ If you are hoping to improve student outcomes through this professional learning, who are the students who expect to benefit?
- ☐ What would it look like if you were successful? Could you list four key things that you would be able to see if you were successful?
- ☐ When will you spend some time diagnosing the students existing behaviour or work in detail?
- ☐ Can you collaborate with anyone in planning, evaluating and refining this?
- ☐ Do you know where to look for expertise in choosing an approach?
- ☐ Is there planned time for this to take place?
- ☐ Will you be able to share this with colleagues?

Checklist for a member of support staff working with students

- ☐ If you are hoping to improve student outcomes through this professional learning, who are the students who expect to benefit?
- ☐ What would it look like if you were successful? Could you list four key things that you would be able to see if you were successful?

☐ When will you spend some time diagnosing the students existing behaviour or work in detail?

☐ Can you collaborate with anyone in planning, evaluating and refining this?

☐ Do you know where to look for expertise in choosing an approach?

☐ Is there planned time for this to take place?

☐ Will you be able to share this with colleagues?

Checklist for general support staff

☐ What is the need that you are addressing through your professional learning?

☐ If it is new knowledge, when will you apply it and how will it benefit your role?

☐ If it is changing your regular practice, when will you spend time practising, adapting and embedding this?

☐ Is there anyone you can collaborate around this to support you in taking this forward?

☐ Will you be able to share how you find it?

Further reading

Timperley, H., Wilson, A., Barrar, H., & Fung, I. (2007). *Teacher Professional Learning and Development: Best Evidence Synthesis Iteration*. Wellington, New Zealand: Ministry of Education. http://educationcounts.edcentre.govt.nz/goto/BES. – One of the leading summaries of the research about professional learning from Helen Timperley et al.

Guskey, T. R. (2000). *Evaluating Professional Development*. Thousand Oaks, CA: Corwin Press. – A classic book by Thomas Guskey.

Evaluating the Impact of Continuing Professional Development (CPD). http://webarchive. nationalarchives.gov.uk/20130402123207/https://www.education.gov.uk/publications/eOrderingDownload/RR659.pdf. – A classic paper by Goodall et al. exploring how schools can practically evaluate impact.[11]

Notes

1 Kruger, Justin; Dunning, David (1999). Unskilled and unaware of it: How difficulties in recognizing one's own incompetence lead to inflated self-assessments. *Journal of Personality and Social Psychology. American Psychological Association*, 77 (6): 1121–1134. CiteSeerX 10.1.1.64.2655 Freely accessible. doi:10.1037/0022-3514.77.6.1121

2 Wiliingham, D. T. (2012). *When Can You Trust the Experts?: How to Tell Good Science from Bad in Education*. San Francisco, CA: Jossey-Bass. http://public.eblib.com/choice/publicfullrecord. aspx?p=827129_0.

3 Lemov, D. (2010). *Teach Like a Champion: 49 Techniques That Put Students on the Path to College*. San Francisco, CA: Jossey-Bass.

4 Seleznyov, S. (2017). Improvement through lesson study, *Teaching Times*. https://www.teaching-times.com/news/improvement-through-lesson-study-ttr.htm. Accessed 19 November 2017.

5 Wiliam, D., & Leahy, S. (2014). Sustaining teaching learning with teacher learning communities, *Learning Sciences Dylan Wiliam Centre*. http://www.dylanwiliamcenter.com/files/pdf/Sustaining-TLCs-20140829.pdf?aliId=89372614. Accessed 19 November 2017.

6 Timperley, H., Halbert, J., & Kaser, L. (2014). A framework for transforming learning in schools: Innovation and the spiral of inquiry. *Centre for Strategic Education*. https://educationcouncil.org.nz/sites/default/files/49.%20Spiral%20of%20Inquiry%20Paper%20-%20Timperley%20Kaser%20Halbert.pdf. Accessed 19 November 2017.

7 DuFour, Richard, Eaker, R., & DuFour, Rebecca (2008). *Revisiting Professional Learning Communities*. Bloomington, IN: Solution Tree Press.

8   Coe, R. (2013). *Improving Education: a Triumph of Hope over Experience*. Cem Centre. http://www.
cem.org/attachments/publications/ImprovingEducation2013.pdf. Accessed 24 December-2017.
9   Guskey, T. R. (2000). *Evaluating Professional Development*. Thousand Oaks, CA: Corwin Press
10 Teacher Development Trust (2017). CPD Quality Framework. http:// tdrust.org
11 Goodall, J., Day, C., Lindsay, G., Muijs, D., & Harris, A. (2005). *Evaluating the Impact of Continuing Professional Development*, Research Report 659, Department for Education and Skills.

four
Culture
The make or break for professional learning

We were recently interviewing a teacher, Sadia, about her experience of professional learning. She described it like a fairy tale … but we weren't so sure.

Before we met her, Sadia had spent her first two years of teaching at a tough school. It was on its fourth headteacher in as many years, with struggling exam results and huge pressure from the local government. This pressure was felt keenly by the staff in the school - Sadia described it as a 'bruising' experience.

When Sadia and her colleagues got any time for professional learning, it was entirely focused on a word that she'd come to dread: 'consistency'. In this case, this word meant lots of prescriptive procedures for all teachers to follow. Sadia described frequent, no-notice 'drop-ins' where senior managers would appear with a clipboard to monitor compliance. Student data was scrutinised frequently, and one bad set of results could lead to a teacher being put on a 'support plan'.

Last year, just over a quarter of the staff had left. While some staff, including Sadia, were able to progress in their careers, there was a culture of fear and uncertainty.

When visiting schools, we look at how the work culture supports learning for teachers and other staff. Do teachers and their colleagues feel that learning is exciting and engaging? Do they feel a sense of belonging, that they are trusted, nurtured and given the time and space to grow and develop? What Sadia described to us didn't come close.

Sadia then enthusiastically explained how she had just moved to a different school which she described as 'worlds away'. This new school is a large high school where students are achieving amazing results. The staff turnover is low, and Sadia was bubbling over with good things to say about the level of support she receives. She described how the senior leadership of the school work hard to ensure a balanced workload – they value their staff and see professional learning as a key reason behind their high retention and high morale in the school. Sadia and colleagues feel valued and invested in. They are supported to earn various accreditations, they often engage in developing their subject knowledge and there is a wide range of professional learning available.

There's no question that Sadia is much happier, and we certainly were pleased to hear that. Yet, as we listened to her enthusiastically describe the huge menu of things she and her colleagues were doing, we realised that something else was missing. The list of what everyone was doing was vast. Great energy was being invested with everyone zooming around and dipping into all sorts of experiences that they found fascinating. But nothing seemed to connect. They talked about 'what I find interesting' but we couldn't pick up patterns that suggested there was a coherence behind all this enthusiasm that would ultimately help students.

Rather than seeing professional learning as a key driver behind best meeting their students' needs, Sadia and her new colleagues seemed to view it as something enjoyable that broadly improves their thinking – it was certainly interesting, but it was hard to see how this lovely new knowledge linked back to the classroom and students. Because the new knowledge wasn't being applied and wasn't closely linked to her students, Sadia found that, as soon as things got busy for students with exams, then professional learning fell off the radar because, despite being interesting and exciting, it wasn't important enough to her day job and the genuine challenges she faced.

Where the first school was a flock of sheep being harried to follow a narrow pathway, the second school was a shoal of very energetic fish – all swimming around happily and energetically but with little apparent overarching direction.

Whilst both of Sadia's schools were extremes, what they show is how the culture of professional learning, or the culture of a school, can really impact on its success. It is 'the make or break for professional learning'. In struggling schools, teachers feel isolated or divided. In successful schools, teaching is a collective endeavour, with every student benefiting from the combined wisdom of all staff.

In visiting lots of schools, we have seen virtually the same structures look wildly different in different contexts. It's difficult to pin down what makes a culture, and yet we can see how important it is. This is a real challenge; culture is crucial to the success of professional learning but slow to change and hard to define. Yet, effective professional learning also contributes to a positive culture; it enables increased confidence, self-efficacy and improved morale amongst teachers. Culture and professional learning form a virtuous circle.

This chapter will explore different aspects of processes around professional learning which contribute to a positive and supportive culture. Some are quite standalone, and some are closely linked, each will likely look different in different contexts, but all will contribute towards an environment where teachers thrive and children succeed.

The organisational 'edge'

In the introduction, we defined the organisational edge as the place where the staff and systems of the school interact with the students, parents and community. Imagine a school as a circle. All the staff, leaders, policies, procedures and systems lie within the circle, the students, parents and communities lie outside, and the edge of the circle is where the interaction between staff and systems and students, parents and the public take place. This edge is the important line, where impact is created through the interaction with the outside world. The centre of the circle – all the leadership, the systems and resources – ideally supports the organisation to be effective at its edge.

The edge represents teachers in classrooms. It represents the conversations and emails with parents. It represents the interactions between adults and students in corridors and on playing fields. It's the complexity of real life: students, families and communities.

Schools are incredibly complicated places. No two students are the same, no two parents are the same. The complexities are ever-changing – as anyone who has worked in a school will know, change can occur incredibly rapidly. The organisational edge is where the organisation must respond to the greatest complexity and change. It is the part of the organisation that is closest to what is really happening, where the nimblest responses can be enacted.

Life on the edge needn't feel like life on a *cliff*-edge, however. A great organisation and a great organisational culture empowers those working at the organisational edge to:

- develop the best-possible understanding of those they interact with;
- build a deep understanding of who and what they are dealing with;
- have clarity about what they can and should achieve;
- flexibly and adaptably use the best tools, resources and approaches to create successful long-term outcomes; and
- collaborate coherently with each other in pursuit of the above.

Professional development is key to enabling those interactions at the organisational edge to work best, empowering staff to build the knowledge, practices and tools that can help them to help students. Any developmental culture ought to be focused on supporting teachers and staff to flourish at this edge and to empower them to be evaluative practitioners, constantly checking 'have I made a difference yet?'.

To build this culture driven by the needs of the organisational edge, there are three key themes that repeatedly appear both in research and when having conversations with teachers. These are:

- Trust and mutual respect
- Prioritising and resourcing professional learning
- Communication around professional learning.

This chapter explores each key theme in more detail and then explores some key building blocks for developing from a poor culture to a developmental one. Finally, we review performance management and appraisal, processes which link particularly closely to culture.

Trust and respect

Imagine trying to learn when you don't trust the people around you. Why would you take on a difficult challenge when nobody is going to step up to support you? We wouldn't tolerate this for the students in our classrooms; we shouldn't allow it in staffrooms either. In great schools, teaching is a collective endeavour. Colleagues are 'there for each other' and the team thrives by learning from difficult challenges.

The importance of trust and respect – a look at the evidence

There's a large literature on the importance of a positive working culture for teachers.

Perhaps the best-known research was carried out by Bryk and Schneider in the late 90s and early 2000s, when they studied four hundred elementary schools in Chicago over four years. They found that the levels of trust between staff was a key factor in whether the school improved. While a handful of schools had high levels of trust and remained ineffective, almost none of the low-trust schools improved at all.

Bryk and Scheider found[1] that high-trust schools had more collective decision making, were more effective at implementing change and found that change was driven by everyone, not just a few leaders. They found that the two key factors behind increasing trust were:

1. Principal leadership: school leaders who listen, acknowledge vulnerabilities, match words with action and maintain consistent goals.
2. Community engagement: encouraging teachers to build relationships with parents.

Kraft and Papay[2] found that teachers in a supportive environment were significantly more likely to be improving their effectiveness over time. On the other hand, teachers working in an unsupportive culture not only improved effectiveness more slowly in early career stages, but then tended to plateau. This is a depressing finding – despite all that hard work and effort, they were getting no better at helping the young people in front of them.

Kraft and Papay identified six factors that correlated with whether teachers improve year-by-year, which included[3]:

- School culture – the extent to which the school environment is characterised by mutual trust, respect, openness and a commitment to student achievement and success at the organisational edge.
- Principal leadership – the extent to which school leaders support teachers and address their concerns about school issues, focused and driven by priorities at the organisational edge.

In earlier research, Johnson, Kraft and Papay found that whilst a multitude of factors influenced job satisfaction for teachers, trust, respect and openness were vital aspects of culture in schools that were improving.[4] They found that responsive leaders that addressed teachers' concerns were also factors that were likely to positively affect student outcomes.

Viviane Robinson's seminal research on school leadership describes three key school leadership capabilities and five key school leadership dimensions which are 'student-centred', focused on what is needed at the organisational edge.[5] The three capabilities are:

1. Integrating educational knowledge into practice – constantly finding the best expertise and knowledge and integrating it into every aspect of the way that the school works. Leaders are committed to nourishing every person and process with wisdom, scholarship and ideas.
2. Complex problem-solving – embedding a commitment to relentlessly find, explore and fix problems and overcome barriers. No stone is left unturned, no problem buried, no barrier left unchallenged.
3. Building relational trust – developing exceptional teams and effective communication to give an environment filled with openness, integrity and mutual respect.

In the pressures and busyness of school life, building trust and respect can easily slip down the priority list. Yet, this research clearly shows that a culture of trust and respect not only helps staff satisfaction but is also important for student success and for supporting the best possible outcomes for children.

Some ingredients of trust

What makes us trust each other? In any relationship, we constantly assess whether the other person is acting in a way that will affect us (or those we care about), and whether that effect will be positive or negative. Factors that we will be assessing may include:

- Social standing: are you enhancing my standing in the eyes of others, or do you risk humiliating me?
- Agency v. restriction: are you enhancing my control over my situation and future, or are you constraining my ability to succeed or escape unpleasant situations?
- Fairness: are you acting in a way that I perceive as fair, equitable and just, or are you sowing discord and division?
- Competence: do I assess that you are likely to succeed, reducing our shared challenges and producing shared success, or are you likely to increase risk and challenge? Do I perceive that you think that I am capable, or do you expect me to fail?
- Predictability and integrity: am I confident that I know how you are likely to react or am I on edge that you behave unpredictably or erratically? If you say that you will do something, am I confident that you will follow through?
- Relatedness v. alienation: do I feel that we have shared values and outlook, that you feel like 'one of us'?
- Authority: what level of power do you have over me, physically, mentally or socially? The more power that you have, the more cautious I will be and more alert to possible threats as they can escalate more quickly.

School leaders always carry their authority with them, whether they want to or not – it comes hard-wired to the position because they usually have the ultimate say in key decisions on hiring, firing and pay. Any action or message will be interpreted in much more detail and others will always read between the lines (not always correctly) to try and guess hidden intentions. While every member of staff in a school has an important role to play in building trust, leaders have a disproportionate influence in increasing or reducing it. It is important to consider these ingredients and how you might be reflecting them.

Leadership driven by the organisational edge

Schools are filled with informed and passionate individuals. They are exceptionally busy places with many competing priorities and, sometimes, external pressures. There are often competing pressures in a school and, of course, sometimes there is disagreement around desirable outcomes. Even in the most successful schools you cannot avoid this. However, where there is a shared purpose, trust and respect between colleagues, these disagreements can be healthy and even productive. Diverse views can help reach the best solutions, avoiding group-think and embracing the complexity that practitioners face when working at the organisational edge.

This doesn't mean that teachers and leaders will always have the answer. It doesn't mean that every strategy works first time. Yet, where there is a shared goal and where staff and leaders both trust each other to have the right outcome in mind, any mistakes or changes in direction contribute to a learning culture, rather than take away from it.

Leaders with a relentless focus on the organisational edge tend to:

- Describe how every initiative and policy links to student success and shared goals.
- Stop doing things that aren't supporting student success.
- Be unafraid to change their practice in light of new evidence, they have a constant focus on improving to best meet their students' needs.
- Explicitly talk about everything in terms of students and the organisational edge and deliberately choose not to refer to any other competing pressures from inside the circle.

- Consistently focus on supporting colleagues to have high levels of agency, competence and security in their work at the edge, in the pursuit of success and reduction of stress or threat.

A consistent focus on improvement at the organisational edge has many positive social and cultural influences. It ensures that finding solutions for students is prized, recognised and esteemed. It demonstrates a feeling of purpose that all staff can recognise and buy into, more than merely complying with procedures or being friends with the right people. This in turn improves the sense of fairness. It improves staff members' sense of agency and increases relatedness through shared goals and focus. Certainty is increased as colleagues develop a shared sense that everything is focused on empowering them to help students.

Modelling

An edge-focused organisation with a culture of trust requires more than just talk. It requires leaders to 'walk the talk' and ensure that they visibly demonstrate the shared goals and values.

Leaders should demonstrate how they deal with the challenge and vulnerability that comes with teaching and professional learning at the complex organisational edge. This takes leadership beyond nice words: talking about the importance of the organisational edge could be lip-service, but modelling working and learning at the edge demonstrates its importance. This is why it is helpful for organisational leaders to be seen spending time with students, families and community rather than being sat in an office.

For many leaders, this may come through a regular teaching commitment. This allows leaders to share an aspect of teaching with which they're struggling and publicly inviting support and input from others. They could ask colleagues to observe them teach a tricky lesson where they would value feedback and an extra pair of eyes to evaluate student responses. It could even be as simple as sharing their own development areas with colleagues and talking about how they are addressing them.

When introducing a new policy or procedure, leaders can build trust by being amongst the first to whom it applies. For example, leaders could announce that they're trialling a new marking and feedback policy in their own classes, share their own honest experiences of using it and be open to hearing others' experiences. A new 'open door week' could be led by leaders who very publicly invite colleagues to observe their classroom, allowing their vulnerability and their openness to learning to be visible. A new appraisal process could be trialled with more senior colleagues offering to be subject to it and inviting other key colleagues to be the appraisers.

School leaders who still spend a significant portion of their time teaching and teaching well are often respected for this by colleagues, as long as they are clearly subject to the same standards and policies. Similarly, senior leaders need to show that they understand the difference between teaching a couple of classes a week compared to having a full timetable of teaching. Many teachers we have interviewed speak very positively about any Headteacher or Principal who is still teaching and, importantly, still developing their teaching. It is not so much the act of still teaching that helps leaders be respected by their colleagues, it is also the process of working alongside and sharing challenges. As mentioned later in this chapter, the risk of resentment that leaders do not understand the demands and time constraints of being a teacher is high. Mitigating this by working alongside one another and still teaching, still developing one's practice can be very helpful.

Finally, innovation and experimentation are key areas where modelling can play an important role. Professional learning relies on focused experimentation in the classroom and then evaluating, refining and adapting practice. This process needs to be explicitly fostered and celebrated, as there can be an inclination to stick to what you know. Where leaders can model their willingness to innovate and take risks, as well as evaluate them, other teachers tend to be more willing to engage in similar practices.

Staff wellbeing

When working with people, in any organisation, staff wellbeing should always be an important consideration. Schools are incredibly busy places and have such an important role, that they can easily be places of stress. We must look after the people that we work with.

It's hard to find a common definition of wellbeing. Our suggestion is that wellbeing involves physical, emotional and social domains, with the feeling that you have the resource, security and support in each domain to achieve success for yourself and others.

Wellbeing shouldn't necessarily be equated with happiness. An individual with great wellbeing will still regularly face challenge and frustration but will feel that they will be able to overcome them in the end and feel happy and proud later on. Wellbeing means having a healthy balance of highs and lows, challenges and successes, with the physical, emotional and social resources to 'surf the wave' (Figure 4.1). It doesn't mean preventing any lows or

FIGURE 4.1   Staff need the resources to surf life's wave.

challenges. Indeed, an organisation that looks only at short-term happiness may be papering over bigger issues or reducing the availability of ultimately satisfying challenges. This is as true for students as it is for staff.

Staff wellbeing inevitably contributes to how people are able to perform in the classroom or in their role. Success in professional learning, effective practice, teacher and student successes are out of reach if there are widespread threats and challenges that staff feel unable to deal with.

However, we wouldn't necessarily advocate for professional learning time to be set aside solely for activities designed for a moment of short-term wellbeing. Consideration of wellbeing should be woven through professional learning policies and every school policy. Sticking plaster approaches, such as a one-off yoga session in an after-school session will probably not address any ongoing wellbeing issues – at best they give a short period of respite from the pressures of the day, but on their own they patently fail to match our definition of wellbeing. Worse still, if staff feel that underlying concerns are never going to be properly addressed anything other than superficially, it is damaging for the organisation and undermines any hope of improving wellbeing.

Staff wellbeing should be a thread that runs through decisions. Some key factors and policies you might like to review or consider are:

- Managing workload and competing time pressures. An unmanageable workload will inevitably link to problems with staff wellbeing as it means there is insufficient time to focus on students' issues and it can lead to physical and emotional exhaustion. There needs to be a sufficient opportunity for a work-life balance and in work staff need to be able to devote adequate time on the most important and impactful activities. We give some ideas for reducing workload later in this chapter.
- Developmental appraisal and evaluation processes. As explored in depth later in this chapter, there should be a culture of development, where staff are free to learn from mistakes, free to try things out and learn from them if they don't work, and where any appraisal or evaluation is not too high-stakes and both challenges and supports staff.
- Explicitly refer to wellbeing and workload in new policies and initiatives. Token references to workload and wellbeing are unhelpful if they are not backed up by real support. However, explicitly referring to how wellbeing is a priority, modelling your own work-life balance and being open to and taking seriously any feedback or concerns around wellbeing and workload promotes an environment where staff are more likely to thrive.
- Careful consideration around key transitions, such as new staff, parental leave, sick leave or any personal challenges. Prioritise flexibility and support for these colleagues.
- Ensure that you have clear processes for someone who is concerned for their wellbeing. Each member of staff should know where to turn and be confident that they will get help. One school we work with has a clear protocol and appoints wellbeing leads to achieve this. Staff members there are confident that action will be taken to address concerns.
- Ensure that you have clear processes if someone has concerns for a colleague's wellbeing. Again, it must be clear where to turn and how to raise the issue. Not dissimilar to referring a child protection concern, some schools have a clear process for who to report any teacher wellbeing concerns to. It clearly indicates that

wellbeing is something that is considered, is recognised as a priority, and that it is ok to talk about.

Powerful professional learning is not only important for student success and effective practice, but it also supports teacher wellbeing. EPPI-Centre research from 2003 showed that effective professional learning can lead to greater confidence amongst teachers, greater self-efficacy and greater enthusiasm and willingness to try new things and innovate in their practice.[6] Leaders who combine a rigorous commitment to reviewing and managing workload, who enable a supportive and developmental culture and provide powerful opportunities for development and learning for their staff will enable an organisation that best supports wellbeing. Of course, there should be processes for wellbeing concerns, but don't forget how wellbeing is inextricably linked to development, learning and time.

Quality dialogue

At the heart of an effective organisation is high-quality communication. Great conversations can increase relational trust and mutual understanding. On the other hand, poor communication will undermine organisational success.

Listening

Quality communication begins with listening and understanding. Any message can be communicated more effectively if you understand your audience's needs, challenges and values. Problems can be more effectively solved when more perspectives are taken into account.

The most successful schools, therefore, gather perspectives and views carefully from every member of staff. There is huge power in engaging with the combined wisdom of all staff, rather than using only senior leaders' views and external data to plan school improvement. A neat and tidy senior-leadership spreadsheet can rarely reflect the true complexity of the families and students with which teachers are working. Schools should be driven to meet the needs of the organisational edge and therefore they need to be well-informed of the realities of what's happening there, rather than by the policies, data systems and processes in the centre.

There are a number of ways we've seen schools ensure that they are listening to staff:

- Surveys – these are used most commonly but they must be used carefully. We have probably all experienced 'survey fatigue' where we don't bother to answer surveys properly because we are just bored of completing them, where we can't see the relevance or where we can't properly fit our feedback into the limited options presented. Similarly, it's easy to get a small number of responses from an unrepresentative group which doesn't tell us as much as we need to know and risks giving a false sense of security that all views have been taken into account.
- Focus groups – focus groups and open forums to discuss key issues can be very helpful. It is worth making sure these include a range of staff with different roles, experiences and from different parts of the organisation. Be aware of which staff aren't able to attend these, or actively choose not to – you may need to solicit their opinions in other ways and their reasons to not attend may be important.
- Using team and middle leadership meetings as a way of gathering information from different parts of the organisation. This relies on there being an open culture and

effective communication within each team, so shouldn't be used exclusively, but is an important role for a middle leader; collating and feeding back the views and needs of their team.

■ Teaching and learning teams – we have observed that a number of schools built a group of staff from all areas of the school whose job is to ensure that professional learning is always responding to staff and students' needs.

■ Bottom-up planning sessions – some schools have managed very effective ways of gathering input from all staff and using a whole-staff session to discuss findings. This works best when partnered with other tools, so that you start the session with particular focuses based on previous input, rather than having too broad a discussion to be purposeful.

Removing defensiveness

It is a huge problem in any organisation if people become entrenched in their views and defensive in their interactions. This is a danger for all of us. When we have worked hard on anything or feel passionate about an issue it is easy to feel that any discussion of it implies criticism – these are examples of the psychological biases described in Chapter Two: the fundamental attribution error and the sunk cost bias. This is just as true of senior leaders as it is of other members of staff. Defensive conversations are rarely useful for professional learning – they can become personal and emotionally charged.

Defensiveness builds up when the key trust factors are seen to be broken. It builds up most rapidly when those with authority are seen to break them!

When there is an air of defensiveness in a school, people often avoid potentially challenging conversations. This allows resentment to build up as there are always issues that are unaddressed and opinions that are not shared, leading to everyone reading (or misreading) between the lines suspiciously. Things move from bad to worse as difficult issues remain unaddressed and communication breaks down.

This is an area where perception does equal reality. And it is one where there will be misunderstandings based on small things. It is therefore crucial that leaders work hard to address defensiveness. In the next sections, we describe some of the elements that need to be deployed by all staff, but particularly by leaders.

Open conversations

One key to removing defensiveness is to use a more open style of conversation based on coaching principles.

Coaching is a highly skilled profession. We offer a few introductory approaches in the hope that our wise readers understand that this is merely the start of a long journey of developing expertise. Coaching is a common area in which the Dunning Kruger effect exists – 'I've read a chapter on this and now I'm an expert'!

A coaching structure for conversations

This structure can be helpful in a formal problem-solving meeting when one person is actively working with another to help them find a solution to an issue.

1. Helping to identify and clarify the most pressing issue that needs resolving.
2. Reflect on implications: what is the current impact and what would the future look like if:

   a. nothing changes; or if
   b. the issue is perfectly resolved.
3. Identify sources of new expertise, new perspectives, new thinking to shed new light on the issue.
4. Identify a powerful first step and commit to it.

The ladder of inference

When dialogue is ineffective, both parties spend more time thinking about what they are going to say next and only listen superficially to the other's points, jumping rapidly to conclusions which inform their preparation for their next statement.

The first shift is for each person to get better at active listening. This happens at two levels:

1. Listening to the words of the other person and stopping yourself getting lost in your own preparation for your next statement. It also requires actively limiting and filtering your own contributions to only the most valuable ones for the current conversation.
2. Watching body language and facial expressions of the other person, listening to the *way* they express their points and carefully considering and reflecting on their mood and motivations, reading between the lines of what is being said. It also requires consciously controlling your own body language and facial expression to put the other person at ease, to empathise with them and acknowledge their feelings.

The first level is hard to do and the second level even more so. But active listening means spending more time actively trying to extract meaning and motivation rather than preparing what you're going to say next.

To assist in the analysis of what others are saying, it's worth reflecting on how we all jump to conclusions. Based on the work of Chris Argyris,[7] the ladder of inference is a useful tool to explore the way we find meaning in what we see, hear and feel.

1. *We select facts or data*
   - We filter the things that we see and hear based on what we're paying attention to, what seems familiar or what we're interested in. We tend to gloss over or actively reject the unfamiliar or challenging. This can happen consciously or unconsciously.
   - Our emotions can restrict our ability to 'cast the net wide' and take everything in – we 'amp up' some facts and 'drown out' others while our nerves are jangling. In particular, we pay disproportional attention to perceived potential threats or rewards.
2. *We interpret the facts*
   - We assign meaning to items of evidence based on our mood, our previous experience, culture (organisational, personal, national, etc.) and understanding. We superimpose feelings, meanings and ideas that may not have been intended by the original speaker/author.
3. *We draw conclusions*
   - We summarise our filtered, re-interpreted data and select a conclusion.
   - We then focus our attention on the conclusion and tend to allow the data and interpretation process to fade from memory – our limited conclusion feels more like established fact.

We're prone to reach conclusions that conform to our existing views, filtering and interpreting the data to help us achieve this. Challenging views which may lead to us feeling embarrassed or angry tend to result in us drawing a conclusion that the other person is hostile, unreliable, untrustworthy, etc.

For example, someone I line manage notices that I ask a different colleague to carry out a task that would normally be his to do.

He's feeling tired and anxious about his own performance and comes to the mistaken conclusion that I don't have confidence in him anymore.

Within just a few days, all he remembers is a that I gave a task to someone else because I don't trust him – he's forgotten that he came to this conclusion based on very limited observation (he could have missed something important) and that there could well have been many other interpretations.

He's 'climbed up the ladder of inference' based on his existing views and perceptions and interpreted something uncertain to align with his existing thinking that our relationship is poor.

This is a common issue where there are low levels of trust between two people. On the other hand, if we like someone then we cast even unreasonable data in a more favourable light, reaching less negative conclusions. We may choose to minimise or water-down any conclusion, and pussy-foot around its presentation to avoid presenting data that we believe could harm our relationship.

Once we reach a conclusion, we tend to cling to it. However, most people reach conclusions while missing a significant number of other views, interpretations and facts.

A key role of coaching-style conversation is to interrupt the process of jumping to conclusions and walk the coachee gradually 'down the ladder of inference' to re-examine filters, interpretations and conclusions. This can help them to see that there are multiple conclusions that can reasonably be drawn when a similar set of observations are interpreted from different perspectives and experiences.

This ladder of inference is also useful when expressing your own views. For example:

'John told me that he had been offered the new role and I noticed that I had not received an email about it. I interpreted that as you deliberately not offering me a chance at the new role. My conclusion is that you think there is something lacking in my performance or potential. Have I missed something, or interpreted something incorrectly?'

This is a much less defensive and aggressive approach to making an otherwise difficult point and allows the other person to identify different facts or perspectives that may have been missed.

Generally speaking, coaching-style conversations are solution-focused, i.e. they are designed to try and reach a better situation. This is opposed to conversations focused on 'winning', i.e. proving your point or demonstrating your ego more powerfully than the other person. Part of the process of being solution-focused is actively listening to different perspectives and opening your own sets of assumptions for questioning. It also requires each party to respectfully acknowledge each other's emotions.

When done well, these sorts of conversations can reduce a sense of unfairness and increase relational trust.

Six useful questions for leaders adopting a coaching style in conversation

1. What's on your mind? *A powerful question for initiating conversation which signals your curiosity, openness and readiness to listen.*
2. Let me check I've understood. Are you saying <re-phrase and summarise>? *This is a great way to check that you've really heard and understood what the coachee has said, and a great way to play back ideas to the coachee to help them clarify them.*
3. You've said you think <X>; could you tell me what you've seen and heard that makes you think that? *This can help the coachee explore how they reached a particular inference, often discovering that it was weaker than they had thought.*
4. What's the real challenge for you here? *Encourages the coachee to move beyond a laundry list of anxieties or concerns and reflect on the root issue.*
5. It sounds like you're frustrated/disappointed/angry about X. In your ideal vision, what should X really look like? *This question re-focuses on goals and positives and helps a coachee imagine light at the end of the tunnel.*
6. Who could you ask to get a new perspective on this? *This helps a coachee realise that there may be more than one way to look at a situation. It also avoids you, the coach, slipping into mentoring or teaching.*

Co-planning and co-construction

Successful organisations value perspectives from colleagues with all levels of experience, from all parts of the organisation. In approaching any problem, some colleagues will have more direct contact with the issue while some will have more background knowledge about it. Different colleagues may experience the same issue or situation and interpret it differently.

For example, if a teacher is working day-to-day with a student with a low reading age, then they may have a different set of perspectives than the SEND coordinator who barely knows the student but is an expert in the issue. To come up with an effective approach, it is vital that there is some kind of co-constructive process.

Complex organisational problems are typically solved more effectively where different perspectives can be valued, shared and compared.

Do's and don'ts for building a culture of trust and learning

A school culture that fosters trust between and with colleagues, where staff feel listened to and free to give and receive feedback, where everyone feels that they are working towards a shared goal to meet students' needs will enable professional learning to flourish. This type of developmental culture is not only likely to be a more pleasant place to work, but also will support your students to succeed, too.

Do

- Constantly link back any policies or strategies to the expected benefits they will bring at the organisational edge.
- Listen to staff, encourage honest feedback and use surveys, focus groups and other feedback routes to ensure that there is open dialogue.
- Celebrate innovation and new ideas and the learning that comes from them, even if they don't work.

- Develop high-quality conversations and dialogue at all levels of the organisation.
- Consider how leaders' actions support social standing, agency, fairness, predictability/integrity, competence and relatedness.

Don't

- Refer to any external pressures from systems, policies or leaders, everything should be driven by the needs of students, teachers and parents working at the organisational edge.
- Forget to be aware of and try to defuse defensiveness. It's often a natural and instinctive reaction in all of us.

Prioritising and resourcing professional learning

In a successful school that is driven by the needs of the students, families and communities at the organisational edge, professional learning will be a big priority. Professional learning enables a happy workplace with good retention, but it is also vital for students' success by ensuring that teachers are drawing on the best ideas, the collective wisdom of their team and of the experts to whom they are connected. Yet, if staff members are to believe that professional learning is valuable, they also need to see that their leaders value it. Powerful professional learning requires time and resources. This chapter explores four key ways to prioritise professional learning, through demonstrating its importance, managing workload, providing time and providing space.

The importance of prioritising professional learning

Viviane Robinson described five key school leadership dimensions, which are 'student-centred' focused on what is needed at the organisational edge.[8] These include:

- Environment – protecting time for teaching, learning and professional development by reducing external pressures and interruptions and establishing an orderly and supportive environment both inside and outside classrooms. This dimension recognises that no learning and development can occur when classrooms are, for example, disrupted by poor behaviour or where teacher time is sucked up with bureaucracy, monitoring and accountability. This also involves re-balancing priorities so that the focus is on the organisational edge, not on processes that face inwards.
- Resourcing – aligning the commissioning and deployment of resources, time and staff to the highest priority teaching and curriculum goals. It includes recruiting, developing and deploying the right staff members. It includes prioritising those things that will have the greatest impact at the edge of the organisation, on the largest number of students.

In this section, we unpick how leaders can demonstrate that professional learning is a priority and describe actions they can take to maximise time, space and resource for it.

Modelling

Earlier in this chapter, we reviewed how leaders can build trust by modelling their own policies and potentially exposing their own vulnerabilities. But this modelling – making leaders' own professional learning visible through talking about it and showing it – does more than just build trust. It reinforces the importance of professional learning to the organisation. When leaders make their own professional learning visible, it helps establish it as a priority. *Modelling* of professional learning includes:

- As a leader, talk about *what* you are currently learning, *how* you are learning it and *why* you are learning it. E.g. *'I'm currently trying to improve the way I introduce isosceles triangles. I noticed that quite a few of my students are struggling so I've been reading guidance from the National Centre for Excellence in Teaching Mathematics and I've asked the maths subject leader to help me implement it in my planning. Next week she is coming to observe the lesson with me and we've designed a diagnostic assessment to learn more.'*
- Talk about your failures and struggles as well as your successes – both the process and the more emotional aspects. E.g. *'I once had a really tough year 10 science class where I struggled with behaviour. I admit that I really doubted myself and I suspected that others were doubting me too. It was tough to ask for help but a huge relief when I started to work through the problem – I think it might have been the hardest but most valuable professional learning I ever did.'*
- Be clear on the tough choices you've made to make your learning a priority. E.g. *'At a couple of points in my career I had to make difficult choices to make sure that my learning was really effective. I held back on leadership training and applying for senior leadership until I had completed my Master's. I didn't want to do either of them half-heartedly, despite being ambitious and wanting to progress.'*
- Be present in professional learning sessions – make sure that senior leaders are 'lead learners' in sessions where other colleagues are expected to learn, being an example to others without dominating the session.

If leaders do not show how they prioritise their own professional learning, colleagues are unlikely to do so. It can contribute to an open culture of dialogue. Of course, modelling certain practices can be a successful mechanism *within* professional learning, particularly when developing novices, but here it is the cultural impact that is important.

To paraphrase Dylan Wiliam, 'every teacher should improve, not because they must, but because they can' – this applies to leaders too![9] Engagement and trust is more likely to build when leaders demonstrate their vulnerability, share their practice, learn from others' practice, share what they wish to develop and be open to collaboration. Too often leaders of professional learning spend most professional learning time delivering to others, rather than modelling their own learning.

Some important risks to look out for around modelling professional learning:

- School leaders missing professional learning time due to competing pressures. This sets an example to colleagues that other things are more important, that being a manager means that you need to learn less than others.
- Appraisal and monitoring processes that reduce trust and create undue stress. We all need space to try out things that might not work. Ensure that any monitoring processes that apply to teachers also apply visibly to leaders.
- Talking about your own learning but not listening to others talk about theirs. We are all novices and experts in slightly different things. We all have the opportunity to engage in new and wider ideas and we often have lots to learn from each other, regardless of experience.

- School leaders avoiding uncomfortable ideas and perspectives while expecting teachers to embrace them. For example, expecting teachers to reflect on whether some of their teaching practice could be better without being open to discussion about whether some aspects of their leadership could also be better. It's important for leaders to show how they are open to challenge and difficult ideas.

Managing workload

Even where people understand the importance of professional learning, it often feels less urgent than other tasks. How are you managing and reducing competing demands? There are often barriers that need to be removed for professional learning to flourish.

We occasionally hear teachers or staff talk about professional learning being 'one more thing on their to-do list' or how they feel that they should be marking assessments or planning lessons rather than developing themselves. One teacher we met described how sad he was that he didn't engage in professional learning more, but he felt that he needed to 'preserve time for himself and his family somewhere'. Teachers and schools are almost always short of time.

Fulfilling bureaucratic needs in the centre of the organisation can all-too-easily crowd out a focus on supporting those at the edge. Similarly, the need to continually deliver activity at the edge of the organisation can crowd out time to improve the quality of that activity.

Effective professional development is embedded in the day job. It requires weekly opportunities to reflect, collaborate, evaluate and apply ideas. It needs regular time to engage with ideas and expertise.

However, if you add in more professional learning time, you must remove the need to spend time on other things. This not only allows more time to be used for formal professional development but leaves mental space for more informal reflection, discussion and reading.

We've worked with many schools who have worked hard to tackle excessive workload. Here are a few of the strategies that we've seen in multiple schools. Some of these are also referenced in more detail in England's Department for Education Workload Reports.[10]

Quick wins	■ Some student self and peer marking of work instead of teacher marking. ■ Using marking codes or symbols to designate common feedback points instead of writing out feedback long-hand, then presenting a key at the start of the next lesson. ■ Push administrative briefings into emails, use team meeting times for professional development discussions. ■ Shared behaviour follow-up systems: e.g. shared detention times.
Medium wins	■ Using more online automatically graded assessments, e.g. online homework systems and multiple-choice assessments. ■ Arrange for fewer staff briefings and meetings and/or replace these with professional learning discussion time. ■ Developing comprehensive schemes of learning and associated banks of high-quality resources and assessments which take much less time to turn into bespoke lessons. ■ Require fewer whole-school data entry points each year. Consider using administrative staff to do physical data entry or try and capture data automatically. ■ Carefully review how teachers use parent meetings and report-writing: these can easily end up as highly time-consuming activities that neither teachers, students nor parents particularly value.

Big but tough wins	■ Reducing teaching loads so that there is more time available each week.
	■ Hiring more staff to allow staff to be more regularly and flexibly released from regular teaching and other roles.
	■ End the school day earlier one day each week and give dedicated, protected time to professional development.
	■ Reducing mandatory non-teaching duties such as supervising break-times.

A really useful starting point is to have a workload working group, made up of a mix of staff of different role and seniority, to regularly review how staff members are spending their time.

Any feedback and marking policies or data tracking should be purposeful and manageable, so that they inform Responsive Professional Learning, rather than hindering it. Any data that is collected should be manageable and have a clear purpose that is beneficial to teachers and students, rather than equating quantity of feedback with quality.

Leaders should maintain a consistent and close eye on workload. Use leadership time to frequently talk to members of staff about what has taken up their time that day and be aware of that ever-common gripe – leaders forgetting how busy full-timetable teachers are and how inflexibly they are able to allocate their time.

Time for professional learning

Having reduced other workload, how can you find time for professional learning?

Schools are always pushed for time and money. Finding time or making time for professional learning are probably the things we get most frequently asked about. The first thing to consider is what sort of time are we looking for?

Activity	Nature of time needed
External courses and visits	Time out of school to explore conferences, listen to speakers and speak to others. This could be for one-off events that fit within a longer programme, or for more regular, structured inputs or study programmes.
Internal training sessions	Formal, protected time for delivery from experts or peer-to-peer presentation of ideas.
Collaboration time	Protected meeting time for structured discussions, co-planning, co-assessment.
Co-teaching time or observation time	Time in the classroom for the delivery/facilitation of a lesson and observation of the students' reactions to it.
Individual reading and reflection time	Sufficient time for researching, reading, reflecting and writing about professional learning.

Every member of staff needs time for all five types of activities listed above. Yet, even when these things are acknowledged, it can be very difficult to plan for.

There is significant variety in how much time and resource is provided across schools. Recent research by the Teacher Development Trust suggested that there are a few hundred schools in England that have zero or near-zero budget for professional learning spending, whilst at the other end of the spectrum there are hundreds of others that spend over 1% of their budget on it.[11] When looking at time for professional development, across thirty-six international jurisdictions, the Education Policy Institute found that the average number of days per year spent on certain types of professional development varied from forty (Shanghai) to 2.8 (France).[12] (It suggested the average was ten days for the USA and four for England.) Obviously, this suggests the national policies and systems play a significant role in this, but even within England alone we see vast differences in teachers' opportunities to access learning for themselves.

Schools that most effectively build in professional development tend to use multiple approaches to finding time. They then protect it carefully, avoiding letting the inevitable deluge of urgent day-to-day activities eat into this important time.

Finding time for professional learning

Here are some of the ways that we've seen schools re-engineering school schedules in order to create opportunities for professional development. Not all of these will work or even be seen as acceptable in every institution and many of them need careful discussion with staff, parents and students. Nevertheless, it's useful to see the range of approaches taken.

Quick wins	■ Schedule music, sport, art, reading sessions and/or religious education with external facilitators.
	■ Staffing assemblies with fewer staff and/or teaching assistants and external facilitators, freeing up others to meet and discuss pedagogy.
	■ Allocate statutory in-service training day time for Responsive Professional Learning, co-planning, discussion and enquiry.
	■ Ask a few classes to come in for a small part of a school-closure training day so that a few lessons can be undertaken with several teachers and/or observers.
	■ Schedule student trips with more (suitably prepared) volunteers and fewer teachers, use the released time for professional learning.
	■ If there are common tests/assessments, sit them together in larger groups, free up other teachers.
	■ Schedule demonstrations, singing, plays and videos in larger groups.
Medium wins	■ Extend team meeting times to encourage subject-specific or topic-specific professional development discussion instead of time spent as a whole staff discussing general pedagogical principles.
	■ Disaggregate statutory in-service training days, use the time instead for several twilight or dawn sessions. Be aware that there's an important balance to be struck here to ensure that teachers still have sufficient planning and preparation time at the start of term as well as time for key activities such as moderating coursework.
	■ In secondary schools, use freed-up time after exam groups have left. In primary schools use Year 6 secondary-visit days.
	■ Arrange for community service or work experience days, or half-days.
	■ Schedule online revision or interactive learning sessions, supervised by an assistant, or sat in larger groups.

Big but tough wins	■ Schedule teacher non-contact periods so that groups can work together (e.g. phase teams, subject departments or faculties, year teams).
	■ 'Bank' fifteen to thirty minutes of extra professional development time by finishing school lessons slightly later on four days of the week and then using that time on the fifth day – e.g. pupils arrive later than usual, or leave earlier than usual.
	■ Schedule similar classes together (e.g. KS2 literacy periods, Year 10 maths) so teachers can more easily swap classes or see each other's lessons, and more easily engage in joint planning and assessment.
	■ Schedule two staff to the same class to facilitate co-teaching.

Cover (i.e. releasing the normal class teacher)

- Use senior leaders' time to take over classes. This has the added benefit of helping senior leaders to familiarise themselves with a wider range of students.
- Combine some classes in the hall or other larger space, using one teacher and/or a teaching assistant or cover supervisor.
- Some schools use higher-level teaching assistants and/or cover supervisors to take classes. This is, perhaps understandably, a more controversial approach and other schools we've worked with insist on fully qualified teachers in front of every class.
- Hire an in-house cover supervisor (or share one between smaller schools).
- Once some cover capacity has been found, give teachers cover 'tokens' which they can use as they wish, subject to availability.

Making collaboration time more efficient

- Use video to allow teachers to record lessons to observe later. We generally recommend that this is mixed with in-person observation as the experiences are quite different. Video also needs more time in follow-up meetings to watch the clips. High-quality audio is particularly important to understand what's going on.
- Create and implement clear and efficient protocols and practices for collaborative meetings, for example:
  - Be clear on the focus of any collaboration and be quite strict about not deviating from it.
  - Be explicit about what you won't cover in a collaborative meeting – it is so easy to go off on a tangent or get stuck on one thing.
  - Share the agenda beforehand and give colleagues enough notice to bring the relevant work or resources to the meeting.
  - When introducing collaborative meetings, stick closely to any recommended timings for several sessions before deviating from them. This needs very effective facilitation and chairing.
- When co-planning lessons, consider planning and observing a segment of the lesson rather than the whole thing. For example, this could be around the first ten minutes, or around a key explanation or activity. This also reduces the challenge of

releasing a class teacher to observe – someone can step in for a few minutes while they watch the short lesson segment.

- When co-planning, don't feel the need to start writing a lesson from scratch every time – staff members can re-use existing plans, schemes and books. Spend time focusing on adapting it for the specific students and focus of the professional development.
- Keep writing-up time to a minimum – don't insist on too much paperwork and encourage staff to identify what write-up is most important.

Watch out for common pitfalls of introducing more time

- Some staff may find it hard to flex their start and end times due to childcare duties.
- Part-time staff may not have that day as part of their contract. If they are only working two or three days, then the professional learning time will be a disproportionately larger part of their working week than for full-time staff.
- If the school has not had a strong professional development culture, nor high expectations of professional development, many staff may not see the benefit of additional time and may see it as a bureaucratic burden.
- Similarly, well-intentioned senior leaders sometimes try to impose lots of change without much consultation and end up entrenching opposition from union representatives.
- Some schools use a lot of existing meeting time for very strictly defined professional development activity. This can leave teams with insufficient times to deal with day-to-day issues and implementing changes, particularly if there has been inadequate time to get used to reduced time for administrative discussion.
- Watch out for reserving large periods of time for professional development and then ending up repurposing a lot of it to deal with issues that crop up during the year such as running intervention classes.
- Where staff have dedicated meeting time it's important to reduce the chance of interruption and disruption. Teachers sometimes report to us that professional development meetings times are often impossible due to a stream of interruptions from students (or colleagues!).

It's often best to start with the meeting time that already exists. Many administrative and briefing pieces of information are shared during meeting times, and not necessarily to staff who need to be aware of it. It can be worthwhile to scrutinise how existing meeting time is used and to restructure them to be focused on student and teacher needs. The last chapter explores further how to structure professional learning time, including a team meeting.

Physical space for professional learning

Professional learning is a multi-faceted process, much of which takes place within the classroom and some of which may well take place outside the school. Physical space is also something that is often harder to change. However, well-designed working space can enable more productive collaboration[13] and sets a culture where it is a priority that is planned for.

Staff members need spaces for formal meetings, large and small, as well as different flexible spaces for spontaneous discussion. Even corridors can double up as informal places for discussion. Having a well-designed staffroom, or staffrooms within different teams, allows more space and opportunity for informal sharing of practice and discussion around curriculum and practice. It can also be helpful to have two different areas, one for more informal conversation, and perhaps one for quiet working (particularly for staff who do not have their own classrooms or space to work in). Consider adding informal spaces where teachers naturally congregate, such as near photocopiers, coffee machines or near the entrance to staffrooms. This could be a mix of formal desk spaces and informal soft-seating areas.

When expecting colleagues to collaborate more formally (either through coaching, joint planning, or a meeting time), you can enable more productive collaboration by finding an area where there is wifi access, noise is fairly low, and where one is less likely to be interrupted. It is helpful to ensure that meeting spaces are pre-stocked with flip-charts, white boards, post-it notes and other useful meeting resources.

Finally, creating space and comfort adds to a much more positive professional learning environment. Whilst tea, coffee, snacks are not going to make the difference between effective and ineffective professional learning processes, they do add to a more positive environment, where staff are likely to feel valued, comfortable and able to reflect and contribute. One school we visited recently provides free hot buttered toast to encourage staff to come together at break times to spend time chatting to each other. Another school hires out a room in a pub for larger middle leadership planning meetings, providing hot food and refreshments to help people feel more comfortable and valued when sharing and developing.

Do's and don'ts for prioritising professional learning

Do

- Model your own professional learning and ensure that this is a key part of good leadership within your school.
- Carefully consider each aspect of how staff spend their day and analyse whether it really benefits the school and students. Monitor workload carefully.
- Visibly prioritise time and space for professional learning above other things that are less likely to impact on students.

Don't

- Provide time for collaboration that isn't focused. Unfocused collaboration might be nice and enjoyable, or it might be a frustrating way to spend time but either way probably won't benefit students.
- Think that providing time, a comfortable space and refreshments is sufficient. That all adds to a positive culture but there also needs to be high-quality relevant professional learning.

Communication around professional learning

Earlier in this chapter, we described the importance of communication in terms of building trust and demonstrating a shared purpose. In this section we explore how to effectively communicate policies, planning and processes of professional learning, so that all staff see it as key to success for both staff and students. It is not uncommon for leaders of professional learning to bring lots of enthusiasm and excitement but to forget how important it is to communicate clearly around professional learning.

Your colleagues may have had negative experiences of professional learning and may carry difficult preconceptions and prejudices. We have seen some school leaders provide lots of time for professional learning because they see it as a real priority, but then it falls flat because there is not a clear understanding of how that time can be useful and used. Communicating clearly around the purpose and importance of professional learning sets up a culture where development is celebrated and flourishes.

Communicating the purpose of professional learning

A developmental culture, where all staff engage in effective professional learning, relies on all colleagues, teaching and non-teaching, understanding the purpose of professional learning. It is not just to enable promotions or meet accountability targets. It is not there as an add-on or to tick boxes. It should make everyone's job easier; it should support everyone to best meet the needs of the students.

Dylan Wiliam has said 'Every teacher needs to improve, not because they are not good enough, but because they can be even better'.[14] We believe that this is fundamentally important; professional learning is not there as a repair tool or punishment for poor performance, it is there to enable us all to meet our students' needs even better. Professional learning is much more likely to have impact in an organisation where there is a culture of development, a strong understanding of why it is important, and a shared expectation that everyone will want to engage in professional learning.

Here are some things to consider checking whether you communicate clearly the importance of professional learning:

- What language do you use around professional learning? Is it explicitly focused on students and their learning, as opposed to focused on teacher performance measures?
- Do you distinguish between professional learning *directly* focused on meeting student needs versus that which *indirectly* benefits students, such as good leadership? Do all teachers engage in both?
- Are all staff members engaging in professional learning? Teachers, teaching assistants and support staff? Experienced and inexperienced? Do you have a vision about how everyone can be engaged in professional learning? Do you offer professional learning opportunities even to those on temporary contracts and those who have signalled that they are leaving?
- Do you celebrate the learning process, including when things don't go to plan, or does success sometimes go unnoticed (and are failures sometimes punished)?
- Do your appraisal and performance management processes emphasise that learning and improvement is continual or do they (perhaps inadvertently) imply that there is a level beyond which it becomes less important?
- Do you have a model of leadership where everyone can contribute, or do you operate a hierarchical model where managerial seniority is conflated with expertise?
- When sharing plans for professional learning, do you explain the research behind your approach? Do you explain the evidence behind it?

Communicating what makes effective professional learning

It is necessary but not sufficient to be clear on the purpose of professional learning. Schools also need a shared understanding of the *ingredients* and *design* of effective professional learning.

If colleagues expect 'professional learning' to mean engaging only in a course, listening to an external speaker or shadowing another colleague's role, then the job-embedded and most transformative elements of learning are being overlooked. If there is a shared under-standing of what *Responsive* Professional Learning looks like, of how collaborative planning, joint observation of students' learning, and evaluating any innovation in your classroom are fundamental parts of professional learning, then colleagues can maximise the benefits of this.

Teachers are always pushed for time. If professional learning is going to be seen as worth spending their time on, then they need to be clear how it will help them and their students.

Fundamentally, we believe that every member of the teaching profession needs to see professional learning as a high priority – something that helps them to help students, families and communities. It's a process aimed at improving the organisational edge, not boosting bureaucracy in the organisational centre. As a leader, it is much easier if your colleagues are able to help you identify and work towards high-quality professional learning.

Do's and don'ts of communicating professional learning

Do

- Make your own learning very visible – talk about what you're doing and how you are applying the key principles of effective professional learning.
- Weave in frequent references to the evidence around professional learning and why you are advocating for certain approaches.
- Be explicit about the benefit to both staff and students.

Don't

- Take up huge chunks of time explaining the principles of professional learning, weave it in.
- Set different expectations for staff and senior leaders around their professional learning. If it's important then everyone should engage in it.
- Forget to be specific about the purpose behind professional learning. Link back to student need, procedures or awareness, where relevant.

Building blocks for a developmental culture

We have identified three key themes that appear in a positive school culture, we have shown what those look like and how you can develop them. Yet, some schools have poor profes-sional learning cultures, rather than developmental ones.

Changing a poor culture to a developmental one takes significant time. Changing habits and expectations can take several years and there is a journey that takes place. At different steps along that journey you might settle for slightly different priorities.

Here's two extreme examples of different starting points.

Apple Primary – poor culture	Cherry School – developmental culture
Apple Primary has had three headteachers in four years. During that time, the school's exam outcomes dropped considerably below national average. They had an inspection which indicated considerable areas for development. Graded, one-off teacher observations have been used frequently over this time. Professional learning has been a series of one-off briefings about an endless array of new approaches. Staff morale is low and there are high levels of burn-out.	Cherry School has had fairly stable leadership for seven years and they have gradually developed a professional learning culture that is based on research, peer observation, sharing of practice and an open culture. Staff are willing to try new things. They feel confident innovating in their practice, and leaders regularly model and share their own professional learning and areas that they are working on.

If these two schools both wanted to introduce collaborative enquiry and Responsive Professional Learning into the schools, they would have very different starting points and very different journeys.

It is plausible that Cherry School has a reasonable culture of trust, that colleagues are open to learning from one another and that there is a culture of learning and developing and being open about aspects of practice you might wish to approve. The process of structured enquiry might be new and potentially challenging for many staff, but some of the building blocks are in place and the culture seems quite ripe for introducing that new process.

However, Apple Primary will need to spend time building a developmental culture and increasing levels of trust before introducing a full Responsive Professional Learning process. They might start with a change in approach to observation and how staff are appraised. This would help to change the language of professional learning; it is there to enable us to be better, not because we need to fix problems. This would need to be modelled by leaders, sharing their own areas for development and modelling their own professional learning. Staff members may well be suspicious initially that this is 'just another initiative', so it will take time to get this to embed.

Below are some examples of the different practices that you might need to build up to during the journey from poor to developmental learning culture. This is not an exhaustive list but gives a good starting point for different points on along the journey. It is important to recognise that while co-construction, collaborative enquiry and disciplined risk-taking might be the ultimate goal, on the journey, there will be different priorities to build towards that point.

Point in culture journey	Suggested priorities to work towards
Poor culture	■ Staff are encouraged to try out new things and feel safe even if they don't work. ■ Ask staff members to volunteer (and try and get all leaders) their best professional learning experiences – when were they most engaged, excited and happy about their learning? When did it feel hardest but most rewarding? Share those publicly.

Poor culture	■ All staff feel comfortable sharing ideas from their practice.
	■ Send a small group of staff to look at how professional learning works in other schools to bring back ideas and discuss how to implement them here.
	■ Open door week – all leaders and any other volunteers offer opportunities for staff to drop in to take a look at what's happening.
	■ Leaders model their own professional learning, sharing 'what I'm reading' or 'what I'm trying' and lead the way in any vulnerable processes (e.g. they encourage staff to observe a lesson that they find challenging or new).
	■ New ideas that are introduced are evidence-informed and that evidence tends to be shared.
	■ Offer an anonymous feedback mechanism to get ideas about 'what can we do, or stop doing, to help you teach and help you learn and develop'. Show how you act on feedback.
	■ Staff feel that professional learning is something that is there to help them.
	■ There is an informal culture of talking about teaching and learning.
Half-way house	■ Staff are encouraged to try new things and reflect on the impact of them.
	■ There are processes for staff to share ideas, and then plan together or collaborate to take forward new ideas. Staff collaborate on particular areas of practice.
	■ All observations are seen as developmental and formative. Peer observation is student focused (i.e. the students are observed with a view to helping the teacher, rather than observing the teacher's practice).
	■ Staff discuss and share evidence to inform their practice.
	■ Staff feel that professional learning benefits students.
	■ Staff feel that they have input into the direction of their own professional learning.
Developmental culture	■ Staff are actively engaged in experimenting in their practice and adapting and refining it to best meet students' needs.
	■ Staff engage in Responsive Professional Learning around a student learning need.
	■ Staff are comfortable with constructive criticism and share aspects of their practice that they feel are not working, with a view to gathering developmental feedback and advice.
	■ Observation is used to help teachers evaluate their practice and engage in Responsive Professional Learning.
	■ Staff are engaged in identifying their students' needs and using this to drive their own professional learning.
	■ Staff feel comfortable constructively challenging one another's practice, for example by supporting them in evaluating the impact of their practice on pupils through peer observation, or by challenging the evidence base behind an approach.
	■ Staff engage with evidence to inform their practice, and then in Responsive Professional Learning with a view to embedding, contextualising and adapting evidence-informed practice into their everyday practice.

Sharing practice is a great example of these changes in emphasis. A school where teachers have lots of time for sharing ideas is pretty limited professional learning. Ultimately, you need time, resources, support and challenge to take those ideas and adapt them and embed them into your practice, along with expert input and the opportunity to evaluate its impact. However, if a school is moving on from a poor culture, where staff did not share practice regularly, then celebrating and giving time for sharing practice is very important. Collaboration, constructive criticism and enquiry are probably not possible if you don't have a culture of sharing. This means that whilst sharing practice should not be the ultimate end goal, it is absolutely an appropriate goal for certain points along the journey of moving from a reductive to developmental culture.

A key role for leaders of professional learning is to reflect upon the school culture and plan accordingly, whilst also always planning for how that culture can develop.

Appraisal and performance management

For schools to do the best for their students, families and communities, all staff need to be performing effectively. Over the past few decades in England and elsewhere in the world, the dominant approach to managing teacher performance has moved from fairly informal to a much more prescribed approach. These days, schools that aren't seen to be actively managing the performance of employees are seen to be failing.

The four dominant features of performance management are:

- the setting of goals or targets;
- the appraisal of performance against those targets and also against standard descriptors of performance;
- the provision of support to perform or improve; and
- incentives to encourage performance or discourage underperformance.

In this section we look at some key principles of setting up performance management processes that support professional learning.

Many schools we visit use performance management processes that staff members describe as fairly irrelevant to their practice. We've both worked in schools where the annual review is something you only remember about just before it happens. This type of process obviously doesn't support ongoing performance and, in some cases, can hinder effective performance.

Recent research from outside of education found the same picture across many sectors. Gallup's large research review, 'Re-engineering performance management' found that only one in five people feel that they are motivated by appraisal processes and that, in general, performance management processes don't tend to contribute to improved performance.[15]

Yet, done well, performance management supports staff development and their effectiveness in their roles. Kraft and Papay found that the way that teachers are evaluated was a key factor in whether they improved or not.[16] To be effective, evaluation needed to be objective and consistent and feedback needed to be meaningful and helpful for their teaching practice.

The Chartered Institute of Personnel and Development commissioned an evidence review of what works in appraisal.[17] They found that developmental feedback and processes needed to be totally separate from evaluative ones. Understandably, anything that has high-stakes incentives around a person's future career, pay and status can detract from paying attention to the developmental aspects of feedback – the focus will be on performance and avoiding failure. This is analogous to the Assessment for Learning principle that, when students are awarded both performance grades and developmental comments, they tend to ignore the comments and focus mainly on the grades.

This means that developmental observations, developmental feedback from colleagues, regular developmental conversations with your line manager all need to be kept separate from any performance evaluation, particularly if it links to pay or promotion. We would recommend having two separate processes, ideally with two separate people. First, have termly *appraisal* meetings with a colleague who is responsible for any evaluation and any linking to pay, promotion, high-stakes consequence. This focuses on the question 'are you doing well enough?' Separately, you have a line manager, mentor, coach or learning partner who you meet with regularly who provides feedback, developmental conversations and supports your learning. This focuses on the question 'what can you do to improve?' as well as 'how can we help you towards that?'

There are challenges with this, especially in small organisations. You might not have enough colleagues for this to be feasible. Similarly, it can be challenging to pair people with sufficient knowledge and understanding of each other's roles. It is not uncommon for non-teaching staff in particular to feel that their appraisal is run by colleagues with very little understanding of their day to day role, which can make evaluation and feedback feel meaningless. Nevertheless, even in the undesirable and inevitably sub-optimal case that one person has to play both roles, they should be crystal clear about the purpose of each meeting or observation, and as to how each piece of data will be used, keeping the two processes as separate as possible.

Developmental meetings can reasonably be scheduled within professional learning time, as long as they don't push out time for other processes. However, we'd recommend that the more administrative, high-stakes evaluations and subsequent conversations do not take place in these time slots.

Evaluating teacher performance

In addition to separating evaluative processes from developmental ones, it is important to consider the nature of any evaluation of teachers. This is an area where thinking has advanced considerably in the US and UK in recent years. Coe et al.'s report, 'What makes great teaching?', outlines how there are a number of useful indicators for assessing teachers, but that these should be triangulated and low-stakes.[18] We now know that high-stakes lesson observation judgements are not a good basis for evaluating teachers and can often lead to distorting behaviours. Similarly, reviewing portfolios or lesson plans are not reliable indicators of teacher effectiveness.

Some measures are moderately useful, such as using student feedback and high-quality, focused assessment of student outcomes. Yet, even these require significant caution, with careful checking for biases and very specific and focused assessments.

But does this mean we should get rid of any evaluation processes at all if they're so hard to do? This is a topic that is too large for the confines of this book, but our suggestion is that there should be some evaluation of extreme 'flags' in teacher performance. For example, if there are significant 'red flags' around student behaviour or student data, this should be assessed, and appropriate support should be given or. In extreme cases, it may be that further procedures should be considered around the suitability of an individual to the role of teaching. However, beyond this, for most staff the focus should be on clear and specific goals, regular feedback and developmental, future-focused support. We simply don't have rigorous enough methods for reliably and validly evaluating teachers beyond the extreme ends of performance.

Goal-setting and performance management

The Chartered Institute of Personnel and Development have found that setting challenging goals leads to higher performance.[19] Goal-setting can be a good way of enhancing performance and supporting people in their roles. However, these goals need to be specific and the colleague being appraised needs to already have the knowledge or skills to perform the task.

When goals are complex and when the colleague needs to master skills first to reach them, goals should not be targets to achieve, but should be focused on behavioural and learning goals. Everything that we have described about the process of professional development of a complex and adaptive skill like teaching illustrates how the process requires evidence gathering, experimentation, feedback, collaboration, etc. and cannot be summarised as a simple target.

This has significant implications for schools. *Specific* targets and tasks, such as sharing your approach to marking with colleagues, completing training in driving the school minibus, learning to use the new data system, improving the behaviour in transitions between lessons, are reasonable goals that colleagues can work towards. By having them set as goals, colleagues are more likely to complete them. You may wish to use the SMART target approach – they need to be Specific, Measurable, Achievable, Relevant and Time-bound.

However, more complicated goals should be more focused on effort, learning and improvement. Much of what is entailed in teaching and directly benefitting student outcomes is extremely complex, with many variables and possible factors. As such, when focused on student outcomes, we would recommend setting more developmental goals. For example, a goal might be to 'engage in collaborative enquiry focused on improving students' use of vocabulary', or to 'develop strategies that enable students to write longer answer questions more effectively'. Certainly, any broad outcomes across a whole year group or class should be refined into a learning goal, rather than set as a target that will be linked to appraisal.

School leaders often worry that this sort of effort-goal will be 'fluffy' and just allow colleagues to lower their performance. We disagree. Teachers can and should be held to account for showing how they monitored their own impact on students, and for the lengths they went to in order to improve learning. Ultimately, a combination of factors may mean that results of the teacher's efforts don't show up in external exams, but there can be a suitably rigorous process to ensure that sufficient efforts are being made.

This is a real challenge and tension for schools. The most important goals are too complicated to set as targets in and of themselves. Evaluating staff against those targets in a high-stakes way is not reliable enough. Yet, it is important for staff to develop their practice and to be responsive in how their practice benefits students. This is why evaluative professional learning is so crucial, separated from any appraisal and high stakes consequences.

We do know that some evaluative measures are not reliable enough to be useful. Grading lesson observations is not a reliable way of evaluating teachers. Drop-in observations or book scrutiny can encourage teachers to focus on compliance and 'playing it safe', rather than trying out new ideas. It is important that these review processes which *can* give useful indications about practice are preserved for development and evaluative practice, rather than for high-stakes appraisal.

Active participation in appraisal

For appraisal to support development and performance, the colleague being appraised needs to value and trust the process. Too often, appraisal not only feels clunky and removed from the everyday, but it also unreliable and not valued by colleagues, so the focus is on attempting to demonstrate what has happened in the past, rather than how it will help develop you in the future.

Where those being appraised have active participation in their appraisal, they tend to view the process more favourably and they tend to be more motivated and likely to change their practice as a result. This active participation means that colleagues are listened to, their opinion is heard, and that their feedback and views inform the goal-setting and appraisal that takes place. The focus of any appraisal should be forward-looking. How is the process informing and supporting future practice and actions? The purpose is not to rake over the past, but to build fertile ground for the future.

This active participation should also happen on a regular basis – frequent small conversations rather than irregular or infrequent high-stakes conversations where targets can be forgotten for long periods.

Checklist for reviewing your appraisal

Below are some questions you might like to ask staff to reflect on your current appraisal processes. Make sure you ask a range of different staff in different roles.

1. How much do you feel your appraisal supports your professional learning?
2. How do you feel that your appraisal is focused on developing you for the future, or evaluating your past practice?
3. How much does appraisal motivate the appraisee?
4. How meaningful are the goals that are set in appraisal? Is progress evaluated fairly? Is it clear how goals should be met?
5. Do you feel that the appraisal process leaves space for you to give your opinion and be heard?
6. Is performance management primarily designed to reduce poor performance and inconsistency, or is it designed primarily to increase great performance and encourage learning?
7. Are appraisal processes haphazard and inconsistent or are they fair, consistent and well-understood?
8. Who is the intended primary beneficiary from outputs of the appraisal process: the appraisee, senior leaders or inspectors/governors?

Summary

Let's go back to Sadia. Whilst undoubtedly her second school was a much more positive experience and she had the potential to engage in really effective professional learning, it was also easy to stop doing so as soon as anything else became pressing.

Hopefully the next step for Sadia is to work with her school to reframe professional learning. It is something that all staff within a school should be engaged in not only for their own benefit (which is undoubtedly valuable), but also for their students' benefit as well. By constantly maintaining an inextricable link between professional learning and the students, Sadia's school could help support teachers to thrive and support its students even better.

Further reading

Kraft, M. A., & Papy, J. P. (2014). *Can Professional Environments in Schools Promote Teacher Development?* https://scholar.harvard.edu/mkraft/publications/can-professional-environments-schools-promote-teacher-development-explaining

Robinson, V. (2011). *Student-Centered Leadership.* San Francisco, CA: Jossey Bass.

Barends, E., Janssen, B., & Velghe, C. (2016). *Rapid Evidence Assessment of the Research Literature on the Effect of Goal Setting on Workplace Performance.* London: Chartered Institute of Personnel and Development. www.cipd.co.uk/coulddobetter. Accessed 1 August 2017.

Coe, R., Aloisi, C., Higgins, S., & Major, L. E. (2014). *What Makes Great Teaching? Review of the Underpinning Research.* Sutton Trust. https://www.suttontrust.com/wp-content/uploads/2014/10/What-Makes-Great-Teaching-REPORT.pdf

Notes

1   Bryk, A., & Schneider, B. (2003). Trust in Schools: A Core Resource for School Reform. ASCD. http://www.ascd.org/publications/educational-leadership/mar03/vol60/num06/Trust-in-Schools@-A-Core-Resource-for-School-Reform.aspx. Accessed 26-Dec-2017.

2   Kraft M. A., & Papay J. P. (2014). Can professional environments in schools promote teacher development? Explaining heterogeneity in returns to teaching experience. educational effectiveness and policy analysis. https://scholar.harvard.edu/mkraft/publications/can-professional-environments-schools-promote-teacher-development-explaining

3   Ibid.

4   Johnson, S. M., Kraft, M. A., & Papay, J. P. (2012). How context matters in high-need schools: The effects of teachers' working conditions on their professional satisfaction and their students' achievement. *Teachers College Record*, 114 (10), special issue: 1–39.

5   Robinson, V. (2011). *Student-centered leadership.* San Francisco, CA: Jossey Bass.

6   Cordingley P., Bell M., Rundell B., & Evans D. (2003). The impact of collaborative CPD on classroom teaching and learning. In: *Research Evidence in Education Library.* London: EPPI-Centre, Social Science Research Unit, Institute of Education, University of London.

7   Argyris, C. (1990). *Overcoming Organizational Defenses: Facilitating Organizational Learning.* Boston, MA: Allyn and Bacon.

8   Robinson, V. (2011). *Student-Centered Leadership.* San Francisco, CA: Jossey Bass.

9   Wiliam D., & Leahy S. (2014). Sustaining Formative Assessment with Teacher Learning Communities. Dylan Wiliam Center. http://www.dylanwiliamcenter.com/files/pdf/Sustaining-TLCs-20140829.pdf?aliId=89372614.

10   Department for Education (England) (2016). Workload Reports. https://www.gov.uk/government/publications/reducing-teachers-workload/reducing-teachers-workload

11   Teacher Development Trust (2017). CPD Spending Benchmarking. http://tdtrust.org/benchmarking

12   Education Policy Institute, Sellen P. (2016). Teacher workload and professional development in England's secondary schools: insights from TALIS. https://epi.org.uk/wp-content/uploads/2016/10/TeacherWorkload_EPI.pdf

13   Rose, A (2012). Designing spaces for collaboration. http://tdtrust.org/designing-spaces-for-collaboration-in-education

14   Wiliam D., & Leahy S. (2014). Sustaining formative assessment with teacher learning communities. Dylan Wiliam Center. http://www.dylanwiliamcenter.com/files/pdf/Sustaining-TLCs-20140829.pdf?aliId=89372614

15   Wigert, B., & Harter, J. (2017). Re-engineering performance management. *Galllup.* http://news.gallup.com/reports/208811/re-engineering-performance-management.aspx.

16   Kraft M. A., & Papay, J. P. (2014). Can professional environments in schools promote teacher development? Explaining heterogeneity in returns to teaching experience. educational effectiveness and policy analysis. https://scholar.harvard.edu/mkraft/publications/can-professional-environments-schools-promote-teacher-development-explaining

17   Gifford, J. (2016a). In search of the best available evidence. London: Chartered Institute of Personnel and Development. www.cipd.co.uk/knowledge/strategy/analytics. Accessed 1 August 2017; Gifford, J. (2016b). Could do better? Assessing what works in performance management. London: Chartered Institute of Personnel and Development. www.cipd.co.uk/coulddobetter. Accessed 1 August 2017; Barends, E., Janssen, B., & Velghe, C. (2016a). Rapid evidence assessment of the research literature on the effect of goal setting on workplace performance. London: Chartered Institute of Personnel and Development. www.cipd.co.uk/coulddobetter. Accessed 1 August 2017; Barends, E., Janssen, B., & Marenco, P. (2016b). Rapid evidence assessment of the research literature on the effect of performance appraisal on workplace performance. London: Chartered Institute of Personnel and Development. www.cipd.co.uk/coulddobetter. Accessed 1 August 2017.

18   Coe, R., Aliosi, C., Higgins, S., & Major, L. E. (2014). What makes great teaching? Review of the underpinning research. Sutton Trust. https://www.suttontrust.com/wp-content/uploads/2014/10/What-Makes-Great-Teaching-REPORT.pdf

19   Gifford, J. (2016a). In search of the best available evidence. London: Chartered Institute of Personnel and Development. www.cipd.co.uk/knowledge/strategy/analytics. Accessed 1 August 2017; Gifford, J. (2016b). Could do better? Assessing what works in performance management. London: Chartered Institute of Personnel and Development. www.cipd.co.uk/coulddobetter. Accessed 1 August 2017; Barends, E., Janssen, B., & Velghe, C. (2016a). Rapid evidence assessment of the research literature on the effect of goal setting on workplace performance. London: Chartered Institute of Personnel and Development. www.cipd.co.uk/coulddobetter. Accessed 1 August 2017; Barends, E., Janssen, B., & Marenco, P. (2016b). Rapid evidence assessment of the research literature on the effect of performance appraisal on workplace performance. London: Chartered Institute of Personnel and Development. www.cipd.co.uk/coulddobetter. Accessed 1 August 2017.

five

Support and challenge
Engaging effectively with experts

Expertise: an introduction

Teachers are ingenious problem-solvers. The thirst for knowledge in our profession is powerful; we want to find out how to tear down barriers that our students face. There is incredible expertise across our system, in our schools and in our universities. There are new perspectives on old challenges and there is old wisdom to inform new ideas. How powerful it would be if every child was taught with the collective expertise of the whole system.

But sometimes we can be an isolated profession, working in silos. It can feel lonely with the energy drained out of us as we endlessly reinvent wheels. Sadly, some teachers have settled for lower expectations because they haven't yet seen what is possible elsewhere.

A few years ago, we worked with an inner city primary school, School X, with a troubled history. Over many years it had struggled with results and with unstable leadership. When a new Headteacher arrived, new to the role of headship, she faced significant challenges. The following visit from the inspectors rated School X 'requires improvement' and it came as no surprise. This was a school with low morale and a history of papering over the cracks.

The journey that the school went on from there was an amazing one, with many different stories and moments of change. One particular turning point was on a regular staff training day, when the Headteacher hired a bus and took her staff a few miles away to another school, School Y. School Y had also had its struggles and had emerged with an incredible reputation. With a similar ethos and similar children, this school was achieving amazing things.

Staff simply spent a day shadowing their opposite number, walking around and absorbing the confidence, the excitement. They saw new ways of doing things and saw amazing achievements of students just like theirs. The effect of this was obvious when the day was finished. Staff said, 'if they can do it, then we can do it. Look what's possible, it's so exciting!'

This illustrates the power of new perspectives. Learning about something that you are already doing is challenging and external expertise can play an important part in overcoming those challenges.

Expertise is not only about technical know-how, nor is it just about new perspectives. It plays many overlapping roles.

1. Helps teachers to clarify their own and their students' learning goals through expert diagnosis, evaluation and curriculum knowledge.
2. Provides effective, evidence-based practices and ideas;
    a. makes the evidence base and underlying theories accessible through tools, resources and explanation;
    b. translates the knowledge and practice to make it relevant to the teacher's classes and students.
3. Disrupts existing thinking and beliefs, inspiring new thinking and nurturing enthusiasm, curiosity, ingenuity and professional scepticism.
4. Designs and facilitates effective teacher learning culture and processes, encouraging reflection, strong interpersonal relationships for learning, and Responsive Professional Learning.

Not everything here needs to be done by one person; however, each of these roles needs to be fulfilled in some way if teachers are to learn effectively.

Despite the evidence, a number of schools lack key aspects of expertise in their teacher learning. In our work, we often talk to teachers about their engagement with expertise. Do any of these scenarios strike you as familiar?

- You engaged with some expertise which was exciting and inspiring, and yet you didn't have the support, time or guidance to take forward many strategies and embed them.
- You sat through a one-off session that wasn't helpful for you or your students. With support staff in particular, it's common for leaders to invest in training or consultancy without paying close enough attention to the desired outcomes.
- You went to an excellent course and came back with lots of resources and ideas that are still, months later, sat in the 'for later' pile of guilt.
- You completed an accreditation, sustained project or a Masters' qualification with lots of access to external expertise. You very much enjoyed it and learnt lots, and yet didn't get the chance to share what you were doing with other colleagues and have a wider impact.
- You haven't had much external input for several years, as your school is closing their doors to external expertise (largely due to financial pressure).

None of these situations are rare. We need to reconsider external expertise and how we use it to make sure it is really transforming practice and meeting students' needs. Consider the expertise you and your colleagues have engaged with in the last year and ask yourself these questions:

- How much support, follow up, time and resources have colleagues had to pursue and embed expertise?
- How many colleagues have accessed external perspectives and expertise?
- How clear was each teacher of the desired outcomes and how they will reach those when they've engaged with expertise?
- What type of evidence have the experts, trainers, consultants you've worked with provided about their approach?

What is clear is that the role of expert input is much, much more complex than simply knowing the content. Someone fluent in multiplication doesn't necessarily make an expert arithmetic teacher; someone skilled at teaching multiplication won't necessarily make a skilful trainer of teachers in the topic.

Making use of the collective expertise of our profession is not simple. We need experts who know the what, the how and the why. They should be able to assess what others know and to help them know it better. The first section of this chapter explores the nature of expertise and possible sources of this expertise. We then go on to explore commissioning this expertise, before finally exploring research evidence and coaching, two particularly common and key sources of expertise.

What are we looking for?

In this section, we look at some of the many ways that schools can and should be harnessing expertise – both outside of their institution and networks and also by building expert capacity within the school.

Expert in what? Types of expertise

There's several layers to teacher professional learning and when selecting expertise; you want to be clear on where their expertise lies (Figure 5.1).

Let's look at each layer:

Content

To teach students effectively, you need to be knowledgeable and proficient in the content that you are teaching. This requires expertise around the following things:

- Knowledge of the content including its processes, examples in practice, its links to other areas and where to find out more about it – sources of further expertise, whether there are differing views or controversies, any alternative explanations, etc.
- Skill to complete tasks, problems or processes: not only to fluently produce a quality outcome but being able to identify what you are doing at each stage and why, being able to break down processes into constituent parts and describe as you do

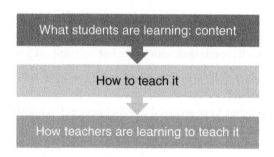

FIGURE 5.1   The layers of professional learning.

- A rich vocabulary to describe the content, its structure and processes.
- An understanding of context: how would the approach used vary depending on where you are, who you're with and what's being demanded.

This is much more demanding than simply being good at a skill, or being knowledgeable about a content area. A great dancer may be able to watch a beginner and identify something wrong in what they're doing. They may even be able to demonstrate it better. But it takes a highly knowledgeable teacher to be able to break down each of the novice's movements and name and explain the mechanics behind each one. Similarly, a highly numerate adult won't typically need to know the names of all the processes they use or remember several alternate approaches. It takes much more than this to be able to teach numeracy.

Expertise can support teachers to develop this skilled content knowledge and understanding.

Teaching and learning: pedagogy

Everyone has come across someone who is an expert in a skill or has expert content knowledge but who is very poor at teaching it. To be a great teacher of the content, we need to build expertise in:

- The process of student learning: not just what is to be learned and developed, but also in what order, and why, what can be expected at different levels, how different types of students will likely progress and why. This includes how content builds on previous content and how it is used to build later content.
- Assessment: how to evidence what students have learned, how effectively and securely they have learned it and to reveal any barriers to learning. This also includes being able to recognise or gather evidence about behaviours to inform the teaching process – e.g. recognise mood, climate.
- Delivery: knowledge of relevant classroom instructions, explanations, tasks, resources for delivering the content. This also includes how to prepare lessons and carry out related tasks.

Expert input in pedagogy can support teachers to best meet their students' needs and enable them to understand the content.

Teacher learning

In the same way that knowing content doesn't necessarily make you a great teacher, knowing pedagogy doesn't necessarily make you a great teacher educator. Experts working to develop teachers (and other staff) also need expertise in:

- The process of teacher learning: what teachers need to learn and develop, in what order, and why, including knowing what can be expected at different levels of performance and competence, how different types of teacher will likely progress and why. This includes how this content builds on previous content and how it is used to build later content. It also includes working with teachers who may or may not yet have strong content background knowledge.
- Assessment and recognition: how to evidence what teachers have learned to do, how effectively and securely they have learned it and how to reveal other evidence about

barriers to learning. This also includes being able to recognise or gather evidence about behaviours to inform the teacher education process – e.g. recognise mood, climate.

- Delivery: knowledge of relevant professional learning approaches, modelling, tasks, resources for delivering the content. This also includes how to prepare lessons and carry out related tasks.

This is, of course, an analogous list to the description of teachers' required expertise.

When looking for expertise, you should be clear about the *type* of expertise that you are looking for and should check whether they have it.

Professional skills

Finally, the ability to teach content and pedagogy is key, but it's just part of the teacher skill set. Teachers also need to be:

- Self-confident, self-aware, enthusiastic and patient.
- Learners: they need to have curiosity, ingenuity, the ability to research and critique, openness to new ideas and different perspectives, a level of professional scepticism and an understanding of research and evaluation.
- Communicators and team-members: listening and questioning skills, ability to explain ideas to students and colleagues, empathy, ability to read others and flexibility.
- Organised: timeliness, the ability to organise and prioritise and the ability to focus and manage distractions are all important aspects of being a teacher.
- Developing leadership and management: ability to inspire, lead others, build and maintain a team, create consensus, make hard decisions, tackle tough issues, develop others and manage upward as well as downward.

Expertise in these areas can support teachers to be as effective as possible in schools.

Where do I find it? Sources of expertise

As outlined in this chapter's introduction, expertise plays four overlapping roles in Responsive Professional Learning.

1. Helps teachers to clarify their own and their students' learning goals through expert diagnosis, evaluation and curriculum knowledge.
2. Provides effective, evidence-based practices and ideas;
   a. makes the evidence-base and underlying theories accessible through tools, resources and explanation;
   b. translates the knowledge and practice to make it relevant to the teacher's classes and students.
3. Disrupts existing thinking and beliefs, inspiring new thinking and nurturing enthusiasm, curiosity, ingenuity and professional scepticism.
4. Designs and facilitates effective teacher learning culture and processes, encouraging reflection, strong interpersonal relationships for learning, and Responsive Professional Learning.

Some of these roles are about content, some about process. Some rely on resources, some on interpersonal interaction. Schools can draw on multiple sources to cover each role.

Below is an outline of various places where you can find this expertise. It is, of course, a never-ending task to outline *every* possible source, but here we aim to give an overview of the important ones.

Higher education

Schools can engage with universities and colleges in many ways.

- Supporting staff to engage in Undergraduate, Masters' and Doctoral-level study.
- Sending staff to seminars and short courses run at universities.
- Commissioning an academic to run a workshop in the school.
- Enlisting the support of an academic to support Responsive Professional Learning projects.
- Collaborating with a university to undertake primary research.
- Collaborating with higher education institution around initial teacher education and ongoing career development.

Higher Education Institutions can play all four roles of an expert. Typically, we find that schools will often initially look to engage around role 2 – explaining and revealing theories, practices and evidence. However, when we ask a group of teachers to reflect on their best professional learning experiences, we often find that they will often focus on role 3 – inspiration, challenge and new perspectives.

Many academics work frequently with schools around roles 4 and 1 – designing effective in-school professional learning processes and helping to identify and clarify goals. This can create an effective collaboration between university and school; it situates much of the professional learning and expert input within the school, so that it is contextualised and purposeful.

In England, some schools partially or fully fund academic study. They will often encourage staff members to focus on an area of study or research which is not only of personal interest but also a school priority. In this way they get double value from the investment: supporting the development of the individual as well as bringing in additional expertise to their school.

Still the most common way for schools to engage with Higher Education Institutions is around initial teacher training. Much of the engagement will be around practical arrangements and support for trainees. This expertise around early teacher development is also a source of expertise and an opportunity for more experienced teachers to learn. For example, some universities will provide training for mentors, or will provide wider support and training to partner schools. Trainees also often convey their new learning and strategies from universities to their colleagues.

Finally, many schools will collaborate with universities and other institutions by taking part in other research projects. The most important benefit of this is to the wider sector. It is vital that the education sector as a whole has access to a wide body of quality research and schools' support is essential to this. However, there are opportunities for further impact and learning for those involved, too. If teacher practice is a focus, there should be a professional learning programme to help develop and embed new practices in the classroom. Ideally, there should also be an opportunity for researchers to share a summary of any existing research and the findings of their research afterwards, supporting schools and teachers to engage in evidence-informed strategies.

When looking for a quality engagement with a higher education institution, it is useful to look for academics who work regularly with teachers and schools. Their understanding of context, effective teacher professional learning and their experience translating academic findings into accessible advice for professionals is invaluable. It can be helpful to work with academics whose work includes systematic reviews and practitioner summaries of topics as well as having engaged in their own primary research. While many schools will benefit from face-to-face engagement with a local higher education institution, we increasingly see technology and social media facilitating much longer-distance engagement around research which can work well, too.

Another way to engage with higher education is for schools and teachers to engage with research papers. We explore this topic in more detail in the section 'Using research evidence to inform professional development'.

School-to-school

Engaging with other schools is an exceptionally powerful way of developing teachers and staff. Staff members will often engage more willingly with ideas from similar school settings than with ideas that sound too abstract and theoretical – it's easier to relate to what is seen and heard in an environment that you can relate to. There are a number of different ways that this might happen, including:

- visits to observe practice – refinements of familiar approaches or highly contrasting approaches;
- working together on planning the curriculum;
- creating local communities of specialist practice to share ideas and advice (e.g. around subjects, roles, or student special needs);
- joint assessment or moderation of each other's work;
- jointly organised training – sharing internal advice, or pooling resources to create a shared internal expert role and/or bring in external expertise; and
- cross-school research projects.

Of these, there are three particularly common ways for schools to collaborate. The first is to jointly commission an expert to come and work with them as a group. This is largely for economies of scale, so that teachers can access input that schools would not be able to afford on their own. This has obvious benefits, although the collaboration between the schools tends to be limited.

The second most common way is through one-off visits to each other's schools. As described in the example at the beginning of this chapter, this can potentially have a huge effect on people's perspectives and sense of self-efficacy. An important aspect of engaging with external experts is to have an outside perspective that helps challenge existing mental models. Visiting other schools often provides this, as well as building awareness, giving practical examples and ideas for how you might change your practice, team, curriculum, administrative systems or almost any aspect of school life.

We easily fall prey to 'halo effects', where everything that an apparently successful school does is seen as similarly effective. Exam or inspection results don't tell you whether the processes within a school are based on the best evidence. Schools are so complex – a school could easily be successful despite one individual poor approach – but we risk assuming that everything a successful school does is effective. Quality consideration, respectful, professional scepticism and critical thinking are important when exploring the practice in other institutions. It's helpful to ask other practitioners about the evidence base and thinking behind their approach, and about how they evaluate impact.

Finally, we see many schools sending representatives to engage in regional meetings for particular roles. Most commonly, this happens at leadership level, where headteachers provide each other with practical ideas, peer support and challenge. Many local areas will also have subject meetings where team leaders will come together to share strategies, to engage with an expert, or to focus on a particular challenge or aspect of the curriculum.

Less common is for practitioners from across schools to collaborate over a more sustained period of time. Timetabling and travel obviously make it harder to manage. We have spoken to teachers who have been involved in projects working with colleagues in other schools and found it very frustrating, finding that there was no shared focus, and that the collaboration was relatively superficial and the overall process time-consuming. However, when done well, the wider perspective and greater opportunities for collaboration are very powerful. This might include teachers coming together around a shared student-focused issue, where teachers can collaborate beyond just discussing evidence-informed ideas, but can peer observe, share examples of work, collaboratively plan, etc. For smaller teams, such as in very small primary schools, a small high school art department or an exams officer, who might not have peers within their own school, this can be particularly powerful.

Perhaps the most powerful potential approach is for schools to work together to develop expertise. We've seen clusters of schools identify individuals to be developed as experts in particular subjects or other specialisms. For example, a group of twelve primary schools who jointly contribute to the time of a teacher in one of their schools to become an expert in teaching geography. This teacher spends two days teaching at their 'home' school and three days working across the other schools. Their work includes developing curriculum and lesson resources, developing high-quality assessment, leading professional development and visiting conferences and leading centres of excellence elsewhere.

Subject/specialist groups

There are many organisations, associations and societies that exist to bring together practitioners and evidence in order to advance practice. Here are some types of organisations with particular examples from England:

- Teacher/School staff associations and unions (e.g. the Chartered College of Teaching, National Education Union, National Association of Head Teachers).
- Subject associations (e.g. the Institute of Physics, the Design and Technology Association, the National Association for the Teaching of English).
- Specialist and role associations and organisations (e.g. National Association for Able Children in Education, National Association for Special Educational Needs, National Association for School Business Management, Teacher Development Trust).

Many of these organisations offer individual or institutional memberships, regular newsletters or briefings or particular services.

We often recommend that schools should look to engage more extensively with such associations – they can be an inexpensive way of bringing the well-informed practice into school, connecting staff members into local and national communities of practice.

Quality assurance of specialist associations can be challenging. Some base advice on the authority of bringing together experience or well-known practitioners, while others take a more evidence-informed approach. It can, perhaps, be easy for an orthodoxy to develop within a professional or specialist association; once the organisation has espoused a certain approach then it may be hard to be objective about shortcomings and alternatives. Some organisations are created precisely because they want to defend or push a specific viewpoint.

We would recommend prioritising organisations with a track record of commissioning high-quality research and relying on well-constructed systematic reviews of evidence. Better specialist organisations will clearly articulate the limitations of any of their recommendations, will tend to avoid tribalism and will focus criticism on ideas and evidence rather than personalities.

Online

There are many sources of expertise available via a web browser or smartphone app. These include:

- Twitter, Facebook and other social media;
- Google Scholar and online research portals;
- Teacher Blogs; or
- MOOCs.

The use of technology and, particularly, social media has opened the doors to more collaboration between schools and teachers. Many Facebook groups allow teachers who probably would not otherwise come across each other to share resources and ideas. Twitter is a fantastic resource for debating ideas, hearing about research and accessing blogs.

However, the real challenge is how to embed these easily accessible new ideas into benefitting practice and students. Much of the expertise available increases awareness and teacher understanding, but to really benefit students, teachers need the support, time and resources to embed and adapt these strategies to fit their classroom. Crucially, they also need to select strategies and ideas that are most pertinent to their students' needs as well, not just ones that look fun or are new and interesting. The 'pick and mix' approach to teaching, where you constantly select new resources and ideas without necessarily embedding or evaluating them, is very tempting when engaging with social media. There is also a greater danger of always being drawn to ideas and practices that are most aligned with your existing thinking, rather than engaging with challenging perspective.

Once again, quality assurance is a real challenge on social media or through blogs. Our recommendation would be to seek out bloggers and commentators who acknowledge their biases, share the evidence behind their approach, look at both sides of a debate and engage in a scholarly way rather than through personal stances.

As well as more opportunities for sharing and building relationships, technology has increased the access to expertise. Google scholar and other online libraries (some are freely available, some teachers and schools pay for access), as well as online courses, MOOCs, etc. allow teachers, support staff and leaders to more easily access a vast range of knowledge and expertise. Whilst this is undoubtedly a benefit to the profession, it becomes more pressing for staff to be aware of their own confirmation biases and how to judge the quality of evidence. With so much more evidence becoming more readily available, there is less reliance on summaries curated by academics and it becomes more important to be discerning and critical in your approach. See our guide to selecting research evidence in the section 'Using research evidence to inform professional development'.

Video

As the cost of good-quality audio-visual equipment reduces, more schools are using the potential power of video to support professional learning. Capturing a lesson on video allows teachers and expert practitioners to explore and reflect later. Clips of video can be much more captivating during training than yet another PowerPoint slide.

Most teachers we meet are very reluctant to be videoed and there is, understandably, a genuine fear of 'big brother' approaches – that video captured will be used by managers as evidence against them. There are now a number of specialist vendors of equipment to capture classroom video which, increasingly, tie absolute ownership of the video to the class teacher. While they can be much more expensive than a handheld camera or smartphone, there can be significant benefits in increased video and audio quality, multiple perspectives and bespoke systems for annotating, storing and sharing clips.

If you are interested in investing in such systems, we'd suggest a fairly slow implementation involving a working party of a range of staff to establish key principles of trust from the outset. Quality of audio can be particularly key for making the resulting clip useful for study.

YouTube, Vimeo and other video platforms increasingly carry clips of practitioners and classes which can be used in discussion. Two challenges here are quality assurance. Is the video showing effective practice? Were sufficient permissions given by teacher, students and parents in order to satisfy safeguarding considerations?

A video can be a very useful way of seeing practice in action but can only ever play a narrow role in providing expert input.

Conferences, seminars and webinars

Lecture and workshop-style input has long been a staple in teachers' professional learning. Watching a skilled presentation of ideas can be a powerful element within a wider professional learning programme. Later, in the section 'Delivering expertise', we describe the important elements of effective presentations.

We would caution against the idea that one-off inputs simply 'don't work'. If you want a process where participants simply become *aware* of a new idea, then a one-off input may be entirely sufficient. For greater depths of impact, a one-off input may sit very effectively if preceded by some preparatory work and followed by time to practise, trial and embed ideas. What is highly unlikely to work on its own is teachers sitting and listening to a couple of hours of input, when the ultimate aim is to change their established patterns of adaptive expertise.

Conferences and exhibitions can be effective ways for teachers to expand their awareness of the landscape in a specialist area. Too often, these opportunities are reserved only for school leaders, but there can be great benefit in a wide range of staff getting time to pick up a greater awareness in their field as part of an ongoing programme of refining and improving their practice, drawing on the best of what is happening elsewhere in the profession.

Tools and resources

An important source of expertise is the curriculum materials that teachers use. This could include high-quality textbooks, where the order of lessons has been pre-structured to align with evidence, where assessment tools have been carefully developed to give maximum diagnostic information and where teacher guidance clearly explains the rationale and evidence behind the choices made.

High-quality curriculum resources and lesson plans can also serve as an important base from which to try varying practice. If a trainee teacher is focusing on improving their behaviour management skills, providing a high-quality lesson plan for them to adapt (rather than re-invent from scratch) can be a helpful support. When learning about something completely new, it is helpful to have guidance and structure.

It's worth noting that we're advocating a set of professional, flexible, expert resources that can be adapted by teachers. We're not advocating a bank of PowerPoint slides and worksheets that teachers must follow slavishly, lesson by lesson. We believe that it's helpful for teachers to avoid being forced to reinvent the wheel and that, even on a day where they have little time to prepare, the resources should allow them to teach a great lesson. However, we believe that these tools need to be empowering and flexible, allowing the teacher to apply their own strengths and talents to the ever-changing and unique set of challenges they face in their own classroom.

Some other sources

While by no means exhaustive, other important sources of expertise can include:

- Students' own perspectives on their own learning – giving important new perspectives into their thinking.
- Parental perspectives on their children's learning, *particularly* where a student has a special educational need where the parent may well know as much as a teacher about the challenge.
- Business expertise on aspects of organisational management.
- Practitioner expertise in subject content, e.g. engaging with artists, musicians, engineers, historians, sports professionals, etc.

Embedding the external expertise internally

It is entirely possible to engage with expertise, make a change in practice, and then rapidly lose the benefit over time. We have a tendency to revert to old habits and existing mental models.

> Almost all reviews found that external input is a common factor in successful outcomes, sometimes in tandem with internal specialists.
>
> *(Developing Great Teaching)*

External expertise is almost always necessary to cause effective change in teacher practice and student learning. However, to ensure sustainability it is also important to develop a level of internal expertise with the theory and practice so that further refinement and adaptation is disciplined by

- the knowledge of what is likely to be more effective;
- an understanding of students' thinking;
- the theoretical basis of the practice; and
- an understanding of effective Responsive Professional Learning processes.

Developing internal expertise to work effectively alongside external experts should therefore be a school priority. This is not only an opportunity to develop a great resource within the school, it's an opportunity to offer exciting development pathways for teachers. For example:

A primary school where one teacher develops a real enthusiasm for science. She is encouraged to join the Association for Science Education and attend regional meetings with experts to develop and enrich the curriculum in this area. Other local schools pay for some of her time to work with their own staff on improving practice in this area.

A high school where a lead pastoral worker develops particular expertise in mental health in young people. He becomes an accredited practitioner and works closely with identified students, but also supports teachers to develop their general understanding and approaches to mental health in their practice.

An internal expert should:

■ act as a conduit between wider external expertise and internal practice;
■ stay abreast of new ideas and practices going on in the wider system; and
■ develop their own expertise in teacher professional learning to facilitate the use of evidence-informed ideas among their colleagues.

Commissioning expertise

As we've outlined, expertise can take many forms, so how do you choose the right expertise? You may be looking for expert content, pedagogy or leadership skills. You may be looking for a one-off course, a conference, a coach, perhaps a series of inputs over time with structured collaborative work between sessions, or perhaps just some material to take away. You might even not yet be sure what you're looking for.

Whatever the form, the quality of expertise chosen will be crucial to successfully reaching your intended outcomes. When commissioning works well, it not only helps schools to get more impact and better value for money, it increases trust from teachers who have greater faith that their time is being well-spent. An effective commissioning process also ensures that expert, teacher and school all get off on the right foot, with clarity of understanding about what needs to be achieved, within what time, and how it will be evaluated.

Start with the end in mind

Effective commissioning begins with a clear idea of what you want to achieve. What is the target of this professional learning and who will benefit?

Target group

What type of impact are you looking for?

Direct impact: Professional learning, which is aimed at the organisational edge, and helps teachers to have impact on their students' outcomes. Most professional learning aimed at improving classroom practice is this type.

For example, your end goal might be success for a specific student, a small group of students with reading difficulties, a whole class, all students from disadvantaged backgrounds in Year 4.

Indirect impact: Professional learning which is aimed at helping the organisation more effectively support practitioners. Developing leadership or support services within the organisation would fit this type.

For example, your end goal might focus on the head of geography, the maths co-ordinator, all the heads of year, the team of receptionists, the catering staff, the senior leadership team or the governors.

Depth of Expertise

What level of expertise are you looking to develop in the teachers or other staff members who are engaging in professional learning?

Level of expertise to be developed		Example
Adaptive practice	High level of expertise and rapid automaticity. The hardest to achieve and the hardest to change once embedded.	Effective management and leadership within face-to-face discussions. Fluency of particular pedagogical knowledge, such as how to answer questions with ease and efficiency within the classroom.
Deliberative practice	Requires the ability to adapt and vary practices but can also draw on other advice. This level of expertise may be a little slower and less instinctive.	The ability to plan an effective lesson in a specific content area or creating a worksheet in preparation for a lesson.
Procedural practice	Rule-following expertise. Sufficient understanding to follow procedure but not to vary it.	System procedural knowledge, such as school policies, systems, resources and emergency procedures.
Awareness	Awareness of ideas with no need to reproduce them or put them into action.	Examples of alternative approaches, wider policies or possible research to change future practice.

Clarity around depth of impact will help you make better decisions about the type, intensity and length of programme you need to design, and who to commission to work alongside it.

Pre-existing expertise and values

The next stage is to consider pre-existing knowledge, skill, habit, values, beliefs, so that you can identify change that is needed. As explored in Chapter One, a complete novice teacher may benefit from being shown clear models of practice, procedures and examples. Yet, most teachers will have some level of expertise or experience which means it is much harder to change and learn. You should consider:

■ Experience: what will participants bring to the table already? This includes existing assumptions about the practices, existing habits, prior experiences (e.g. whether they may have successfully or unsuccessfully tried something before).

- Value alignment: the extent to which an espoused approach or theory will align or conflict with a teacher's existing values, and the extent to which a presenter will be seen as someone they can relate to.
- Belief/confidence continuum: from 'it's not possible for us to do this better' through 'it can be done better elsewhere but not here' and 'others can do this better, but I can't do it better personally' to 'I have the self-confidence and belief this can and will be done better'. Also: 'I don't believe this is the correct approach' through to 'this is ideal, well-evidenced and up-to-date'.
- Trust, willingness to take risks: the level to which teachers feel trusted, empowered and supported to make change.
- Relevance: the extent to which teachers are likely to feel that an aim is relevant and helpful to their aspirations (for themselves, their students, their institution, their colleagues).

By considering these aspects, you take into account multiple perspectives and are more likely to avoid designing something that excites you personally but doesn't work for your colleagues.

Bringing it together

Once you are really clear about your starting point and intended outcomes, you can begin to plan and select the professional learning programme.

Examples

Example 1 A secondary school headteacher wants to ensure that the school is aware of the latest practices and policies around assessment in England's SAT tests for Year 6 (eleven-year-olds). She identifies a colleague who wants to lead on this area but he is not particularly confident in himself while also being sceptical of the new national policies.

The depth that the headteacher is seeking is awareness. It is a specialist field of assessment, and the target group are seven- to eleven-year-olds. The colleague will lead on this area, so it is highly relevant to him, but he is coming with scepticism and low belief.

As a result, the headteacher is comfortable in seeking a one-off conference as this is suitable for fairly high-level awareness-raising. She looks for something with a range of different areas of information-sharing aimed at the relevant age stage (seven- to eleven-year-olds) but also something with an inspirational and encouraging element to build belief and self-confidence.

If she later wants to use the colleague's newfound awareness to implement change, she will plan further deliberative or adaptive learning opportunities if there is significant new learning to implement. This would involve more sustained learning over time with greater engagement with external expertise, and more opportunities to try things out at the school (using the expert input) and evaluate their impact on students and staff.

Example 2 A local government education service has received a proposal to put on a training day around Growth Mindset. Before rushing straight into commissioning, they reflect that the goal here is much more than simply raising awareness of the approach's theory or developing a superficial adoption of new classroom practices – the best that could be reasonably hoped for from a one-off input. After some discussion with schools, they reflect that they need the following:

- **Change in student outcomes**, particularly for those students with poor self-regulation skills who are most likely to give up. This will require a change in **awareness, practices, mental models** and **attitudes** of many staff. All of these will require diagnostic/assessment/evaluation tools.
- **Change in procedures/systems** used in classrooms, interventions, parental engagement, **general pedagogical knowledge** about why poor self-regulation occurs and what to do about it, **specialist pedagogical knowledge** about how to spot and apply this in for different ages, subjects, topics and skills.
- A suitable programme which can **instil a sense of self-belief** in a sceptical and busy/tired audience – some of whom think this is 'fluffy nonsense', that will **differentiate between teachers** for whom this is conceptually new and teachers who feel they have 'seen this all before' or who already know some key principles, and also directly **address leadership issues** within schools where there is high stress/low trust/too little time such that new ideas will be harder to embed.

This process reveals that a one-off session will be entirely unsuitable, insufficient to sufficiently up-skill even the most willing novices, unlikely to overcome lack of school internal time/resource/trust, likely to cause highly superficial adoption of 'top tips' and fail to challenge those who mistakenly think they already do something similar.

Instead they seek to commission an expert or group of experts who can engage in the design and delivery of a longer process which includes group training, in-class modelling, enquiry projects, and leadership/culture support.

Example 3 A teacher has always taught advanced mathematics (A-level, sixteen- to eighteen-year-olds) but he has now been asked to teach a class of eleven-year-old students.

- He needs to develop his **awareness** of the curriculum, assessment and reasonable expectations for eleven-year-olds, as well as awareness of systems and procedures for this age group, including where to find resources/materials, and expected timings of teaching and assessment.
- He also needs to develop **self-belief** that he can work effectively with this age group, overcoming any fears or doubts.
- In order to plan lessons and find/create relevant resources, he will need **deliberative** knowledge and mental models about the acquisition of key mathematical thinking at this age and practices that work most effectively for this age group and for the different topics.
- Finally, to develop **adaptive expertise** of teaching this group, he will need content knowledge, pedagogical knowledge (common misconceptions, curriculum sequences), and general pedagogical knowledge.

As a result, this teacher is seeking some books and resources to build his awareness and deliberative practice, some opportunities to observe really great practice for this year group and mentoring from experienced practitioners as he builds his adaptive expertise.

Commissioning criteria

Once you know what you are looking for, you will need to find expertise that is suitable. There are a number of different criteria to consider before choosing.

Clarity of *needs*: you need to be able to present your needs to a provider of expertise as clearly and specifically as possible.	■ Can you engage the provider at early stages of your planning so that they can inform the process? ■ Are you suitably open to challenge as to whether your desired impact is feasible within the resource available? Are you able to flex your resourcing and thinking to create an effective partnership? It's helpful to work with the provider to identify the best ways to embed any new ideas. You don't want to invest in expertise that then doesn't pay off because you didn't provide enough follow up time and resource.
Quality of *content*: you are seeking content informed by a strong evidence base.	■ Is there a well-evidenced criticism of the approach(es) suggested by different providers that gives a note of caution? Perhaps there's a summary or review of the research to help you? ■ Are any claims being made about good practice (e.g. 'school inspectors want to see this') actually aligned with latest practice/advice or are they rumours or out of date? ■ Is research behind the content provided so that participants can follow-up with deeper reading? ■ Has the content or presenter been accredited or quality assured by a reputable organisation in the field?
Quality of *delivery*: expertise should be aligned with the evidence on effective professional development	■ Are there suitable tools and materials available before, during and after the learning? ■ Is the delivery and service quality assured in any way? ■ Are there independent reviews of the delivery, from previous users/participants or other experts? ■ If there are multiple views being presented – such as different documents or speakers on a panel – then has diversity been considered? Is this provider considering how to represent and promote the views and needs of the full range of backgrounds, or giving only a narrow view?
Suitability of content being presented: advice or expertise needs to be appropriate for the outcome being sought	■ Is it appropriate for the needs of the teachers who will engage with it? ■ Will participants already have the requisite prior knowledge, competency and skill? ■ Is it in a form that is likely to deliver the outcome you need? Are you looking for sustained engagement or a one-off event within a longer programme?
Quality of *service* and *value* for money.	■ Does the provider respond quickly to queries and provide sufficient information at all stages? ■ Are any venues and refreshments of sufficient quality that they don't detract from the experience, and do they cater for the full range of needs? ■ Does the provider respond quickly to queries and provide sufficient information at all stages?

- Are there other genuinely equivalent services, experts or courses which provide similar for less?
- Are any claims of value for money based on a genuine like-for-like comparison of quality and content?
- Can it be delivered in a location that offers value for money? Would it be better to bring the expertise to your school or to send a colleague to a more central location? Could you pool resources with nearby schools and put on a local event?

Evidence of prior *impact*: have there been robust studies of the impact of this advice or expertise on the outcomes which you are seeking?	There is no simple guide to good quality, but the following ideas are likely to suggest better quality: - Multiple studies are usually better than one, especially if they have been carried out by different researchers from different institutions in different contexts. - Studies that use objective, independent measures are probably more robust than those that use surveys of participants. - Studies that are funded by an organisation with a commercial interest in a positive result are likely to be less reliable than those that are independent. - Systematic research reviews of effectiveness that summarise both positive and negative findings of multiple sources of evidence can be very helpful.
Quality of *tools* and *follow-up*.	- Does the expertise come with materials to diagnose existing needs and skills? Are there any preparation activities to help focus participants' minds on the right areas? - Does the expertise come with assessment and evaluation tools to use before, during and after the engagement, to help participants, leaders and facilitators to adjust and refine their approach? - Are there ways for participants to get further or more detailed information about information presented? Can they check on areas of controversy and explore alternative views? - Are there suggested follow-up services, processes and expertise? - Are there suggested organisations and individuals to contact to see the ideas in action, to create networks and to foster dialogue and discussion?

Searching for expertise

You know what you need, and you know what you are looking for in your expert, but where do you find them? A strategic search is important, although the time and effort spent on searching needs to be suitable for the amount of resource expended and impact desired – a brief update on policy for two members of staff needs less time on commissioning than finding an expert practitioner to work with a whole school over the course of a year on literacy for all students.

You could consider:

- What sources of expertise have been used previously by you or colleagues within your institution? Has there been evidence of impact? What independent quality assurance is available to overcome internal 'cosy relationship' biases?
- Who has been used by local individual schools or nearby clusters of school? How did they quality assure the expert and what evaluation did they carry out?
- Who is recommended by leading expert organisations? How do they quality assure?
- Is there expertise provided by a district or regional authority or board? How have they quality assured? Are they able to improve value for money?
- Could you use independent marketplace websites for strategically searching for providers of expertise, such as the *Teacher Development Trust Advisor*?

Using research evidence to inform professional development

Evidence helps us make better decisions. It is an invaluable source of expertise itself and should also underpin all the expertise you engage with. Research evidence can help you understand what has worked, where, why and for whom. It can indicate what is plausibly useful to try and what is less plausibly useful. It can challenge 'common sense' and give us new insights, identify things that 'feel right' but may be less helpful and save precious time, effort and money in the process.

Evidence-informed decision-making is just that – *informed* but without forcing practitioners slavishly and rigidly to follow conclusions. The Centre for Evidence-Based Management identifies[1] four elements of evidence-based practice (Figure 5.2).

This diagram nicely illustrates that decision-making needs to carefully consider values, practices, internal knowledge and context, but should *always* take into account research evidence. The evidence from high-quality research brings with it a level of rigour and independence which helps us break through our significant psychological biases.

FIGURE 5.2   The four quadrants of evidence-informed decision making.

However, this strength needs to be tempered with a few realities about education research. First, for the great majority of decisions that teachers and school leaders must make, there are few relevant studies that reliably point to plausibly better courses of action. Second, the question 'what works?' is a tricky one – nearly everything in education seems to work somewhere and almost nothing works everywhere. What we can do is use high-quality research to point us in directions that are the most plausible bets to try first.

What sort of research?

When seeking out research you need to be mindful of the purpose. These might be:

- Are you seeking experimental evidence to prove **whether** practice X will or will not likely lead to outcome Y?
- Are you seeking theoretical information to explain **why and how** practice X is likely to lead to outcome Y – e.g. the underlying models and mechanisms that help us understand the plausibly best contexts and implementation approaches?
- Are you seeking descriptions of the social, environmental or political **context** in which practice X occurs?
- Are you seeking to understand a **perspective** that is different from yours about a potential recipient of practice X?

Each type of question leads us to favour different research designs. Arguments often rage about which types of research are superior to others without considering the aim. In reality, practitioners are likely to need to be informed about all four of the above purposes if we are going to draw upon evidence to make recommendations.

We would suggest that all schools should develop greater research expertise and engage more regularly with academics and organisations that can source and summarise appropriate research for the questions being asked.

Five common pitfalls

1. **Correlation issues**: This is where a worrying problem is associated with a particular activity or trait and there is a failure to check whether the problem leads to the trait or the trait leads to the problem. For example, 'children who are bored in class are bad at reading'. Is the issue that being bored leads to bad reading? That being bad at reading leads to boredom in class? Or is there a third issue that is leading to both issues? Clearly, identifying a problem the wrong way around could lead to misguided or even damaging conclusions being reached.
2. **Do-something-itis**: There is a temptation to identify a worrying social or educational problem and jump straight to implementing an in-school solution without checking whether it's even possible to solve it in school. For example, 'children appear to have too little creativity' might lead to 'let's teach creativity!' without checking if it is actually possible to teach it in school, let alone how and why it would work. Everyone feels better for doing something, but the school may be displacing useful activities with something that may not work.
3. **Over-rapid adoption**: It is easy to get too excited about early findings or plausible mechanisms and then roll them out as mandatory, without building a quality evidence base and continuing to pilot and evaluate the roll-out.

4. **Filtering evidence by tribe**: This involves rejecting possible mechanisms or findings because of a dislike of the existing supporters or, conversely, holding onto existing ideas too strongly because you and/or your respected colleagues have made a big deal of promoting it. It's easy to recognise this in others but it applies just as much to you or to us as it does to them…

5. **Confirmation-seeking**: This is the inclination to filter research for findings that confirm existing thinking and practice and to pay too little attention to criticisms and doubts. The converse is also true, enormously over-egging fairly fringe doubts about research (or its authors) when it suits us to undermine research that would be uncomfortable to accept.

Ultimately, there is no easy trick to avoiding these pitfalls. A good start is to be aware of them and how easy it is to fall into them. Acknowledge these issues to others. Reasoned debate and discussion, a commitment to good evidence and to furthering the evidence-base, healthy scepticism over both new and fashionable ideas, as well as long standing beliefs, will stand you in good stead.

Improving your use of evidence

One of the most dangerous ways to use research is to read papers, articles or books until something strikes you as exciting or inspiring. A classic example was the excitement generated by the TED talk on 'power poses'[2] that told a great story, resonated with many viewers and appeared to be based on a rigorous study. So many people wanted to believe it and were excited by it that there was little critical analysis, and the idea was adopted into training courses around the world. Sadly, a great number of recent attempts to replicate the original research have failed[3] and it would appear that people have been taking themselves to quiet places to do poses and stretches for no valid reason.

Here's a few ways to get better quality evidence:

1. Look out for systematic reviews. These are studies of existing research literature that are carefully designed to give more weight to higher quality and rigorous research. They identify what it is possible to claim and with what level of confidence. Some systematic reviews include *meta-analysis* – an attempt to combine statistical findings from multiple studies.

2. Be more sceptical of lists of references which are mainly individual studies/experiments. It is easy to pick out multiple impressive-sounding studies to confirm nearly any position that the author or reader would like to be true while failing to reference studies that undermine this. Look for references to reviews of evidence where possible.

3. Search for criticism. Whenever you find a plausible-sounding claim, it is good practice to type it into Google Search and add the word 'criticism' on the end. Other useful words/phrases to add to your search are 'replication' and 'systematic review'. For example, 'power poses replication' identifies all sorts of issues with the initial study.

4. Be even more cautious about individual studies where:
   a. authors do not publish their data and precise methodology for others to re-analyse;

   b. researchers have some vested interest in a particular result, i.e. they lack inde-
      pendence from the subject, they are being paid by an organisation whose products
      they are studying, they are seeking to make profit from their research findings;
   c. big claims are made on the basis of a study of a small number of subjects and/or
      over a small period of time.

Where to find research evidence

Some useful sources of research evidence include:

- UK Educational Evidence Portal – http://www.eippee.eu/cms/Default.aspx?tabid=
  3580
- US What Works Clearinghouse – https://ies.ed.gov/ncee/wwc/
- US Educational Resources Information Centre (ERIC) – http://www.eric.ed.gov/
- Google Scholar – http://scholar.google.co.uk/
- The Education Endowment Foundation – http://educationendowmentfoundation.
  org.uk/toolkit
- The Institute of Effective Education's Best Evidence Encyclopaedia – http://www.
  bestevidence.org.uk/

As a useful starting point, these two lists may also be helpful.

- Professor Rob Coe's list of recommended research summaries and books for teachers – http://www.cem.org/blog/what-is-worth-reading-for-teachers-interested-in-
  research/
- Tom Sherrington's list of research summaries and articles – https://teacherhead.
  com/2017/06/03/teaching-and-learning-research-summaries-a-collection-for-
  easy-access/

Making evidence work in school

Breckon and Dodson (2016) found[4] six key tasks to develop a school (or group of schools) as
evidence-engaged and evidence-informed.

1. Openness – build awareness and positive attitudes toward the use of high-quality
   evidence.
2. Agree – build a shared understanding of, and buy-in to, the key relevant questions
   being asked, and the type of evidence needed to answer them.
3. Access – facilitate access to high-quality evidence and facilitate the effective communication of it at the appropriate times to the right people.
4. Interaction – ensure that researchers, practitioners and decision-makers are able to
   regularly interact.
5. Skills – support decision-makers and practitioners to build the skills to access,
   appraise and make use of evidence.
6. Structure and process – design and refine decision-making and development processes so that using evidence is the norm.

Most leaders and practitioners are unlikely to be particularly excited about the act of using
evidence just for its own sake. Effectively building an evidence-informed culture usually

means starting with what colleagues already aspire to achieve, problems that they worry about solving or finding tools that they will find immediately relevant and helpful.

For most professional development purposes, not every teacher or education practitioner needs to have read the original research. An important school and system role is to identify and develop one or more individuals whose key role will be to stay up to date with the latest research, to find and share research summaries, and to stay aware of the problems or goals that are in school so that the right research can be found.

Individuals and teams in evidence-informed schools tend to have high levels of trust and self-awareness. There must be a culture where decisions can be constructively challenged, and staff feel free to ask for the evidence base. Similarly, staff members need to build awareness of their own biases and trust each other so that these can be supportively challenged at times. Doubt and uncertainty should be celebrated, and statistical literacy needs to be developed.

Evidence-informed schools tend to have a larger number of links to external expert organisations which have a reputation for summarising research and translating it for practitioners. They will typically ensure that there is always a group of staff engaged in academic study in order to build research literacy and increase the links between researchers and the school. They will often commit to engaging in large-scale research studies while also building a local library of high-quality evidence, research and accessible summaries.

Key ideas

- Set up a staff research library which has key research summaries and well-chosen selection of books. Review the selection regularly to ensure that the ideas are the most up-to-date. Provide information about criticism or strong alternative views where possible.
- Set up a journal club which meets every few weeks and where colleagues are invited to read a short piece of a research summary and discuss at the next meeting. Include discussion about methodology and avoid jargon and overly technical language. Include criticisms of ideas as well as exploring the maturity of the idea – how well-developed is the evidence base? Is it working in practice? Is it being superseded? Is there a competing idea?
- Make contact with researchers of key research that you are trying to use in school – this includes authors of systematic reviews. Social media or just email can help with this, academics are often only too happy to provide information or find out how their work is being used.

Checklist

- ☐ We have one or more staff members whose role is to find and translate high-quality research. We invest in developing their research appraisal skills.
- ☐ We engage with expert specialist organisations that provide research summaries.
- ☐ We have a staff library of high-quality research summaries. We seek access to libraries of journals and research.
- ☐ We carefully develop a cautious attitude to the research behind both new and existing approaches.
- ☐ Governors at the school ask for evidence behind policies and strategies.

Putting it together – applying expertise in the Responsive Professional Learning cycle

Expertise plays several roles in the Responsive Professional Learning process that we introduced in Chapter Three. In this section, we look at each stage of the cycle and give some examples of how to work in expert support and challenge (Figure 5.3).

Identify and check: The diagnostic process

In this stage, we're looking to clarify intentions and desired impact, identifying any pre-existing thinking. Expertise can play a number of roles, some of which are listed below.

- Identifying common, high-impact barriers to learning: using research summaries or working with an expert practitioner to look for 'low hanging fruit', i.e. areas of professional learning that are likely to help overcome the biggest challenges for the largest number of pupils.
- Identifying goals: using examples of practice, case studies and descriptions to identify what an ideal outcome looks like, challenging and raising existing expectations.

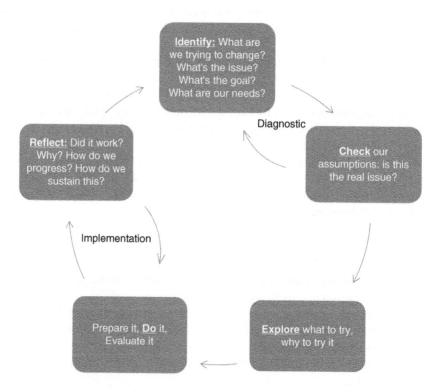

FIGURE 5.3   The Responsive Professional Learning cycle.

- Identifying participant needs: using expert assessments of current understanding, experience, values and beliefs in order to clarify what is being brought to the professional learning process and help to inform the design process.
- Challenge: working with expert practitioners and facilitators who can help to clarify initial goals which may be a little fuzzy, help to identify underpinning assumptions to test. Expert challenge can help to overcome the common problem of participants choosing an intervention or solution before they've properly identified the problem they're actually solving – e.g. 'we're going to improve feedback' without knowing what issue the improved feedback will solve.

In our experience, Higher Education Institutions often have helpful expertise in this area, providing important challenge in the identified of needs and exploring underpinning values and assumptions. If a specific professional learning approach is being used, then there may be specialist facilitators or trainers, e.g. in Lesson Study or Spirals of Enquiry – we've seen many schools struggle to implement effective professional learning by neglecting to engage experts in the professional learning *process*.

Explore the issue

Once participants have clarity about the problem they're solving, they need to explore some plausibly helpful ideas to try. At this stage they need to find:

- What is the evidence about why the particular problem occurs? What's the underpinning theory? This is important to explore in order to come up with a logical and evidence-informed solution.
- Which evidence-informed evaluation tools could be used to diagnose underlying issues? How could these be used to evaluate the impact that participants' learning is having on the target group?
- What are some plausible interventions or approaches to try in the classroom in order to overcome the barriers to learning? How can generic ideas be adapted to specific lessons or for specific students?
- Which tools and resources could be used to support effective implementation and effective professional learning?
- How appropriate are the selected assessments, tools and approaches for this particular context? Is the organisation ready for them? What wider changes might be needed to make sure that they can be fully embedded?
- How settled is the evidence base in the area? Are there existing approaches that are well evidenced and are there plausible innovative alternative approaches? Are there any doubts about the evidence or theory being used?
- Is there any evidence about the best ways to design professional learning for this particular cohort of participants, for this context, for this challenge?

Experts should:

- make sure there is sufficient space to explore participants' existing ideas and assumptions, not just impose their own advice immediately – especially for more experienced teachers;
- provide accessible summaries of evidence in non-academic language;

- be explicit about the weight of evidence and any opposing views;
- encourage critical engagement with evidence; and
- not focus only on research evidence and ignore practitioners and context.

At this stage of the Responsive Professional Learning cycle, most types of evidence can be useful, whether one-off inputs or research papers, expert practitioners or visits to other schools.

Prepare, do and evaluate

In this final stage, experts need to support effective preparation. This might include:

- providing a supportive environment to learn and rehearse any new techniques;
- providing constructive feedback on the rehearsals;
- providing support in the preparation of any lesson plans, scripts or activities;
- challenging participants to be clear on what they expect to happen and how they will evaluate impact.

During the implementation, experts could:

- observe implementation and gather useful information for later reflection; and
- provide in-the-moment corrective feedback or step in to support effective implementation – this should be done with prior agreement and only works with high levels of trust.

Finally, in the evaluation and reflection phase, experts could:

- help to facilitate an effective discussion which is constructive, focused on impact, informed by evidence and avoids detours into unhelpful side discussions;
- reflect back any observations that other participants have missed;
- identify the difference between direct observations and the interpretations that participants add to these;
- suggest future improvements; and
- suggest ways to embed any learning into policies, procedures, tools and materials.

During each phase of the Responsive Professional Learning cycle, experts may find it helpful to consciously adopt a coaching style. In the next part we explore this concept and distinguish between mentoring and coaching.

Coaching and mentoring

Coaching and mentoring are two terms which are often very loosely or inconsistently defined. For the purposes of this book we will use the following definitions:

Coaching is the facilitation of a **reflective conversation** to stimulate **learning and growth**.

Mentoring is **expert facilitation** of a learning process for novices that includes **modelling and exemplification** in order to develop expertise.

We find the two used in a number of places in schools and colleges, such as:

Coaching	Mentoring
Supporting a struggling member of staff to improve	Supporting induction into a new institution
Supporting a member of staff to solve a challenge or problem	Supporting a trainee or newly qualified teacher or other professional
Supporting a member of staff to reflect upon and plan career development steps	Preparing for a leadership role or supporting in a new role
Supporting a member of staff in learning and developing leadership skills	
Supporting a member of staff through a key transition (such as out of maternity or sick leave, into a new key role or into retirement)	
Supporting organisational development	
Supporting regular performance management or appraisal	
As a general style of conversation used by managers and leaders	

Typically speaking, mentoring is a process where an expert is supporting a novice within a domain of knowledge or skill. The expert is known as the mentor, the novice known as the mentee.

In coaching, we are typically dealing with a conversation between the coach and someone who is beyond a novice (the coachee), who has attained at least some level of expertise in a domain. This is because coaching tends to be less directive or instructional and relies more on the coachee reflecting on what she or he already knows.

Does a coach need to be a content expert?

There is much disagreement about whether a coach needs to be an expert in the content they are discussing.

For example, if you know quite a lot about your job, I may still be able to expertly prompt you to reflect even if I'm not knowledgeable about what you do. I would need to be an expert in the process of coaching in order to do that so that I can use emotional cues and skilful questioning in order to make you think hard.

In one sense, knowing nothing about your job stops me from being at all judgemental and stops you comparing yourself to me, allowing you to focus on yourself. However, my lack of expertise means that I can't tell if you are misguided nor if you are stuck in one perspective. I'm unable to provide challenge – that can be both a positive and a negative.

The other extreme is to be coached by a known expert. If you are an expert teacher and want to coach me, then you may be able to more rapidly diagnose and prompt with useful reflective questions. You can point me toward new perspectives and take a view on my existing knowledge. But I may also decide that I simply disagree with your view, or I may not acknowledge your expertise. I may feel that you are being judgemental and may either feel embarrassed and inferior or angry and competitive with you.

No matter which approach is used, what is important is that the coach is an expert in *the process and skill of coaching*. No school should allow the idea of coaching to be associated with poor conversations or misunderstanding. It's therefore useful to make sure that anyone who is engaging in coaching is being properly developed in the process of doing so.

Coaching = dialogue + reflection + relationship

Effective coaching requires high-quality dialogue. The dialogue must include great questions and be carried out in such a way that the coachee reflects deeply on what they are doing and is able to gain new perspectives, or at least better understanding existing perspectives.

Coaching requires a level of openness and honesty; the relationship between coach and coachee is important. It needs to be based on mutual respect.

Great dialogue requires the coach to listen in an open-minded way. Listening carefully includes repeatedly clarifying meaning but also checking inferences that have been made to get at underlying reasoning.

See Chapter Three for some ideas on coaching-style conversations.

Evidence on coaching

Kraft, Blazar and Hogan (2016) find[5] that coaching teachers can have a positive impact on student outcomes. They find that quality of coaching is more important than the number of hours.

Outside education in the more general management literature, a systematic review by Jones, Woods and Guillaume (2016)[6] found that:

- Coaching can be an effective way to increase individual performance.
- Online coaching can be just as effective as face to face coaching.
- More coaching does not mean better coaching.
- Internal coaches are more effective than external coaches.
- The impact of coaching can be *reduced* if the coachee also engages in a '360 degree review' of feedback from colleagues.

Our interpretation of these findings would be that it is helpful for schools to engage with external coaching expertise *in order to develop high-quality internal coaching capacity*.

Coaching within teacher development

Within mentoring

Where mentoring takes place, the aim is to move the mentee from being a complete novice to attaining some level of expertise. This requires a gradual shift from an approach with more modelling and exemplification to a more self-reflective process from the mentee. Mentors need careful training and support to judge the right mix to use. They should also avoid 'judgementoring'[7] (Hobson & Malderez, 2013) – where the mentor either deliberately or accidentally prioritises passing judgement, damaging the chances of creating a safe, supportive relationship.

On the other hand, it's problematic to ask novices to engage too early in self-driven, self-reflective learning. Without sufficient experience and sufficiently well-developed mental models, this can be rapidly overwhelming and result in poor practice developing.

Within leadership

When you become a leader, it is very tempting to use your new status and power to direct others to follow your instructions. The difference in status also makes it harder to really listen to colleagues' views as they feel more at-risk in expressing dissent and you may feel more easily threatened by them doing so.

Intentional use of coaching conversations can help to overcome this. It can help discipline your conversation so that you focus on carefully listening and understanding underlying meaning. It can avoid you jumping to hasty conclusions and help you see situations from colleagues' perspective. Similarly, it can help colleagues think through and reflect on situations.

However, don't confuse this *coaching style conversation* with the expert process of coaching.

Within performance management

Appraisal and target-setting conversations can be significantly more effective when a line manager or appraiser uses a coaching conversation to encourage the appraisee to buy into the process, to become an active participant in their own development and to ensure that there is good-quality communication throughout the organisation. See more on performance management in Chapter Three.

Checklists

For coaches

- ☐ I am constantly seeking out advice and training to improve my coaching.
- ☐ Coaching is seen as neutral and developmental, not only for staff seen as more or less effective.
- ☐ I work to break down barriers of trust, status and communication.
- ☐ I avoid jumping to conclusions and test each level of my ladder of inference (see the section 'The organisational "edge"' in Chapter Four).
- ☐ I help my coachee to explore their conclusions and inferences.
- ☐ I avoid being judgemental.

For school leaders

- ☐ Coaching is seen as neutral and developmental, not only for staff seen as more or less effective.
- ☐ We constantly seek high-quality expertise to develop our coaching skills.
- ☐ We offer training in basic coaching skills to all, without favouritism.
- ☐ We carefully train and support mentors and provide them with sufficient time.
- ☐ We offer coaching at key transition points.
- ☐ We embed coaching conversations within professional learning and performance management.

For governors, boards and trustees

- ☐ We ask school leaders to explain how coaching is being used.
- ☐ Coaching is seen as neutral and developmental, not only for staff seen as more or less effective.
- ☐ We ask how genuine expertise in coaching is being developed.
- ☐ We ensure that sufficient resource is made available for coaching.

For system leaders

- ☐ We offer coaching expertise to schools.

Further reading

Evidence Based Educational Leadership – a blog by Dr Gary Jones (@DrGaryJones) about the use of evidence and expertise in education. http://evidencebasededucationalleadership. blogspot.co.uk/

Using evidence in the classroom: What Works and Why? – Julie Nelson and Claire O'Beirne, NFER. A helpful paper on using evidence in education. https://www.nfer.ac.uk/publications/IMPA01/IMPA01.pdf

Evidence-informed teaching: an evaluation of progress in England – A review by Colwell et al. of how well schools in England are engaging with evidence[8] – http://shura.shu.ac.uk/16140/

What If Everything You Knew about Education Was Wrong? – A book by David Didau (@DavidDidau) to help you question the evidence base of common assumptions.[9]

Notes

1   Rousseau, D., Briner, R., & Barends, E. (2015). Evidence-based management: The basic principles. *Centre for Evidence Based Management.* https://www.cebma.org/wp-content/uploads/Evidence-Based-Practice-The-Basic-Principles-vs-Dec-2015.pdf

2   Cuddy, A. (2012). Your body language may shape who you are. *Ted Global.* https://www.ted.com/talks/amy_cuddy_your_body_language_shapes_who_you_are

3   Morris, David Z. (2016). 'Power poses' researcher Dana Carney now says effects are 'undeniably' false. *Fortune.* http://fortune.com/2016/10/02/power-poses-research-false/

4   Breckon, J. and Dodson, J. (2016). Using evidence: What works? A discussion paper. *Alliance for Useful Evidence.* https://www.nesta.org.uk/sites/default/files/using_evidence_what_works.pdf

5   Kraft, M. A., Blazar, D., & Hogan, D. (2016). The effect of teaching coaching on instruction and achievement: A meta-analysis of the causal evidence. Brown University Working Paper.https://scholar.harvard.edu/files/mkraft/files/kraft_blazar_hogan_2016_teacher_coaching_meta-analysis_wp_w_appendix.pdf

6   Jones, R. J., Woods, S. A., & Guillaume, Y. R. F. (2016). The effectiveness of workplace coaching: A meta-analysis of learning and performance outcomes from coaching. *J Occup Organ Psychol,* 89: 249–277. doi:10.1111/joop.12119

7   Andrew J. Hobson, Angi Malderez, (2013). Judgementoring and other threats to realizing the potential of school-based mentoring in teacher education. *International Journal of Mentoring and Coaching in Education,* 2 (2): 89–108. https://doi.org/10.1108/IJMCE-03-2013-0019

8   Coldwell, M., Greany, T., Higgins, S., Brown, C., MAXWELL, B., Stiell, B., Stoll, L., Willis, B., & Burns, H. (2017). Evidence-informed teaching: An evaluation of progress in England. Research Report. Project Report. London, UK, Department for Education.

9   Didau, D. (2015). What if everything you knew about education was wrong? *Crown House.*

Six

Planning professional learning across a whole year

By now, we've hopefully persuaded you that professional learning needs to be:

- focused on impact at the organisational edge;
- responsively led by evaluative practitioners; and
- drawing on the profession's collective expertise.

In this final section, we present some key tools for putting these ideas into practice.

Fundamental to putting it all into practice is the idea of analysing needs and using those to create a plan for your school. This chapter will explore the principles and factors that need to be considered to put a professional learning plan into place.

It then goes on to further explore particular roles and how they interact with effective professional learning, middle leaders, early career teachers, support staff and governors. We explore how career development and professional learning should reinforce one another. Finally, we outline some key factors of effective facilitation and delivery of professional learning.

The annual professional learning plan

The most successful schools create plans for professional learning that span at least one academic year. This enables a shift in planning, from individual activities to sustained programmes of learning.

An effective professional learning plan begins with identifying aims and outcomes. The activities and programmes then flow from that.

The starting point needs to be analysis of student needs, with the key question: *what do we need to learn to empower our staff to help our students, families and community even more effectively?*

This is consistent with a culture that focuses on the *organisational edge* and not the *centre*. This focus means constantly asking how the school can support, develop and empower those on the frontline – the staff that interact most frequently with students – rather than prioritising the needs of systems, managers or external accountability systems. (See Chapter Four for more)

To achieve this, the professional learning planning process needs to analyse needs from multiple sources of information and for multiple groups:

- Individual staff
- Staff teams and middle leadership
- Whole organisation and senior leadership

Individual needs

This process is best carried out bottom up, starting with the individuals. In addition to their Responsive Professional Learning, individual provision might include:

- Support for individual academic study – e.g. staff working toward an undergraduate qualification or participating in postgraduate study and research.
- One-to-one mentoring and support for staff coping with life transitions or challenge, e.g. returning from maternity leave, managing a mental or physical illness, dealing with a bereavement or major family trauma.
- Professional and career advancement: offering formal and informal opportunities to build a C.V., including work-shadowing, secondments, visits, or professional study and accreditation.
- Individual practice support: expert support for improving specific practices, e.g. classroom mentoring for improving behaviour management, support for someone struggling with achieving a specific accreditation or demonstrating alignment with a set of standards.

Sources of information to identify individual needs include:

- Performance management discussions including regular review of career next steps.
- Teacher self-identification of learning and training needs, including review of own subject knowledge.
- Developmental lesson observations and engagement in Responsive Professional Learning.

Individual needs could be identified through line management and coaching conversations.

Team needs

In this layer you should consider the needs of groups of staff and their particular activity. You should make sure that you include:

- Subject teams: e.g. priorities might include learning about implementing a new curriculum, assessment model, and pedagogical approach.
- Phase, year or age teams: e.g. considering a particular age-related development need for seven-year-olds or fifteen-year-olds, or looking at key pastoral care issues in these areas such as mental health, bullying or attendance.
- Specialist teams: e.g. updates about special educational needs and disabilities, improving practice around trips and excursions, refining practice around data collection and analysis, or updating in the latest practice for stretching the most able children.
- Teams around a specific need or child: e.g. training in effectively supporting a child with a specific educational, behavioural or physical need, for all the staff members who work with them in classes, groups or one-to-one.

- Leadership teams: e.g. developing coaching approaches for senior school leaders, support for difficult conversations for middle leaders, or a programme of work-shadowing for aspiring leaders.
- Career- or job-stage teams: e.g. induction programmes for new staff, support programmes for newly qualified teachers, or train-the-trainer programmes for those who are starting to lead and facilitate professional learning seminars within and outside the school.
- Teaching and technical assistants: e.g. effective one-to-one or small-group classroom support, or training in setting up demonstration equipment in science, art or design technology.

Sources of information to identify team needs include:

- At this level, it is important to amalgamate individual discussions and look for common threads – is everyone in the team struggling with a new policy or system, or does everyone face a common challenge in a new curriculum, for example?
- Joint marking and data analysis, identifying concepts, skills and ideas that could be taught more effectively and then researching ways to tackle that.

Team needs analysis can be supported by external review from an expert from the field. For example, a Year 5 teaching team may find it helpful to get a primary mathematics specialist to support them identifying the most pressing priorities in their development of mathematical teaching.

Whole school

This layer is concerned with the professional learning priorities that everyone in the school needs to consider. This could include:

- Training in new systems or equipment.
- Rolling out a new whole-school approach to behaviour.
- Statutory annual training around health and safety.
- A key priority for the whole school, e.g. the literacy, behaviour or resilience of students.

Important sources of information to inform this layer are:

- Student outcomes review: are there any common challenges across year groups, subjects and topics? Are there overall challenges around wellbeing, attendance, attitudes to learning? This information is amalgamated from discussions at individual and team level, overall trends in summative student outcomes, as well as bringing in any external reviews and other stakeholders (parents, governors and community, for example).
- Leadership and management review: consider whether there are reasonable succession plans and development pipelines for senior and middle leaders; identify any general leadership and management weaknesses from external reviews and staff surveys.
- Inspection reports or external reviews: this external perspective can be helpful (and helpfully challenging) although we would argue that in the most effectively improving schools, inspection grades and reports are not the driving focus for improvement.

- Explore whole staff surveys of 'training and development that I need' and also looks for patterns in reports from appraisal and performance development discussions.
- Review of statutory update: who needs updating in, for example, health and safety training, use of medical equipment or safeguarding.
- Systems and procedures: initial and ongoing training to ensure all staff can use key systems and follow key procedures: e.g. data capture/analysis systems, email systems, computers and projectors, behaviour incident recording and referral procedures and fire safety procedures.

Within each layer you need to give consideration of all of the key groups of staff, typically *teachers, teaching assistants* and other *support staff*. The latter group, support staff, is often the most diverse and hardest to treat as a homogenous group.

Each group will contain roles that contain varying levels of *management* duties. In our view, it is more helpful to see this as less of an end in itself and more of an *indirect* professional learning process, intended to empower teachers and other staff and improve organisational effectiveness *so that* everyone can have more impact at the organisational edge.

Needs analysis: outcomes and depth

As discussed in Chapter Three (the section 'Designing for depth of impact'), we can separate intended outcomes of professional learning into two layers.

Direct impact – focused on the organisational edge. These are activities with an explicit link to student learning outcomes, clear approaches to evaluation and clarity about intended outcomes. In planning this layer you will tend to draw together strands including:

- shared goals and expectations for students by the time they finish at your institution, including what they know, what they can do, how they think, how they are;
- this includes the intended sequence and outcomes of concepts, skills and knowledge while developing self-knowledge and dispositions – e.g. consideration of curriculum and schemes of learning;
- how well current and previous cohorts of students have achieved the intended outcomes; and
- how well these are reliably and informatively assessed by teachers and students, both formatively (i.e. to help students and teachers respond to progress) and summatively (to evaluate and recognise overall success).

Indirect impact – increasing the capacity and effectiveness of the organisation to have impact at the edge. This may include:

- management and leadership;
- awareness of latest developments and research through conferences, seminars, social media, wider reading;
- training in the use of systems and policies;
- statutory updates around student health and safety;
- career development of individuals to support their learning, celebrate their success, develop capacity and ensure that they are encouraged to stay and grow in the education system;
- inspiration or support to raise awareness of what's possible, improve self-confidence, self-efficacy and expectations; and

■ building helpful networks and connections in to gain access to expertise, support, new perspectives and new opportunity.

You should also consider the *depth* of expertise needed:

Adaptive practice	High level of expertise, automaticity and ability to apply flexibly. The hardest to achieve but also, despite being flexible to different circumstances, the hardest practice to change once embedded.
Deliberative practice	Expert practice that can be carried out flexibly with some supports and with time to carefully think through each step.
Procedural practice	Proficient practice that fairly rigidly follows a set procedure or set of rules without significant ability to vary or adapt.
Awareness	A background awareness of the existence of certain ideas without sufficient clarity or depth to yet crystalise into practice.

Creating the plan

Great professional learning needs a plan. But a school is a complex organisation and there are many needs that must be threaded together.

As we discussed in Chapter Three, the basis of a professional learning plan is to consider *programmes*, not *activities* – i.e. start with intended outcomes then thread together the necessarily activities, time, resources and expert input to make that happen.

Pragmatically, any professional learning plan starts with three key elements:

1. The time available for professional learning.
2. The resource (money, expertise, networks) available for professional learning.
3. The intended outcomes of the professional learning.

When finding time, you need to look for five main types:

Activity	Nature of time needed
External courses and visits	Time out of school to explore conferences, listen to speakers and speak to others. This could be for one-off events that fit within a longer programme, or for more regular, structured inputs or study programmes.
Internal training sessions	Formal, protected time for delivery from experts or peer-to-peer presentation of ideas.
Collaboration time	Protected meeting time for structured discussions, co-planning, co-assessment.
Co-teaching time or observation time	Time in the classroom for the delivery/facilitation of a lesson and observation of the students' reactions to it.
Individual reading and reflection time	Sufficient time for researching, reading, reflecting and writing about professional learning.

Pulling this together

We've worked with some schools who use a planning grid approach to ensure that nothing is being missed. The following table is an example.

	Direct	Indirect
Organisation		
Teams		
Individuals		

Ultimately each box needs to bring together:

- Target (e.g. all newly qualified teachers, the Year 3 team, Mrs. Jane Bloggs).
- Intended outcome (e.g. complete statutory post-qualification certificate, improve reading outcomes for students eligible for free school meals, update the behaviour policy).
- Depth of learning, if relevant (i.e. adaptive, deliberative, procedural, awareness).
- Evaluation approach (e.g. tutor observation and portfolio, standardised reading assessments and library records, staff feedback group and behaviour consultant review).
- Professional Learning Programme (i.e. activities, facilitator/supervisor/coach, review point, resources such as time, money, sources of expertise).

In designing the appropriate programme, there are four rules of thumb. The first is that the greater the depth of expertise needed, the more sustained the programme needs to be. Awareness can be gained in a single session, but adaptive expertise takes many cycles of practice and experimentation with expert support and feedback.

The second rule of thumb is that the more existing expertise (i.e. entrenched, automatic habits and thinking), the more useful it is to get participants to lead with experimentation and enquiry. However, the more novice the participants are within a domain of practice or thinking, the more important it is to initially break down ideas into simpler pieces and build up practices as well as thinking with clear models and plenty of practice.

		Pre-existing knowledge, skill	
		No or very few existing ideas and preconceptions $\rightarrow$	Entrenched existing practice/ideas
Depth of expertise sought	Awareness & inspiration	One-off input may be sufficient	
	Procedural knowledge	Multiple chances to observe, practise and get feedback	
	Deliberative expertise	Increasing level of experimentation needed, more sustained, more collaboration and dialogue helpful.	
	Adaptive expertise	Extended Responsive Professional Learning approach over time with plenty of expert challenge	

The third rule of thumb concerns the size of the domain of knowledge/practice being explored. If you are tackling a narrow area, such as the best way to teach students to distinguish between two types of triangle, you need significantly less time spent than on a much broader or more generic area such as *asking questions* or *behaviour management*.

The final rule of thumb concerns attitudes. If teachers already feel confident and interested in a domain of learning, it can generally be tackled more quickly than an area where staff members are anxious, disinterested or resentful. If you feel that any of the latter attitudes are present then much more time may be needed at the outset to try and gain buy-in, build up confidence and build trust. It can also be helpful to ensure that there are more possible early 'wins' in the learning to build positivity.

An important caveat: if you are encountering widespread attitude challenges then it probably suggests that there are bigger issues around leadership and culture. Rather than designing a particularly intensive and sustained programme to force change, it may well be better to first work with staff to identify common ground and get buy-in.

Mapping it into a calendar

The key role of the professional learning planner is to draw together this plan, and continue to balance priorities and resources as short, medium and long-term priorities change.

The final step of the planning process is to map the various programmes and activities into an annual calendar showing all of the slots for professional learning.

In the Chapter Four, we explored some of the strategies that schools around the world have been using to make time available for professional learning activities. As a reminder, these can be grouped into six key ideas:

- Reducing teaching loads or other workloads.
- Early closure or late starts.
- Re-organising in-school meeting times.
- Providing substitute or cover teachers.
- After-school meetings.
- Extending the school year.

When using this time, it's wise to reserve some time slots to leave some room to flex and respond to urgent pressures – don't be tempted to fill every possible time at the start of the year. When identifying your time-slots, make sure you include:

- Formal whole-school training days.
- Shorter sessions run before or after the school day.
- Staff meetings: whole school and team/department/year.
- Line management and performance management meetings.
- Early closure days or late-start days.

Examples of ways to structure time for professional learning

Each of these examples is based on a real school that we've worked with. We've identified key elements of the way they planned their professional learning timetable. We provide commentary on each, along with the ideas we gave them to improve it.

Case study 1 – providing learning time in timetable

In Instance Academy, every teaching member of staff has one hour every fortnight that is timetabled for their professional learning. Teachers decide how to use this regular slot: it can be used for collaborative planning, reflective discussions or personalised research. It is designed to facilitate Responsive Professional Learning. Staff members who share this time together are encouraged collaborate, but little structure is given.

In addition, there are a number of optional professional learning sessions after school which cover key themes identified throughout the year such as differentiation, improving memory or independent learning. These tend to be guided by facilitators, with structured models and suggestions. There are also termly TeachMeets and a celebration evening at the end of the year where staff share their learning from across the year.

Comments   This is obviously a generous and a guaranteed amount of time that many teachers would very much appreciate. For some staff it probably allowed for very powerful collaborative Responsive Professional Learning.

However, some staff would have struggled to find a shared focus for their Responsive Professional Learning and might have found that collaboration was unstructured. Unless very carefully planned and guided, this time could easily have been wasted or perhaps resented by some staff. It could be improved by ensuring clearer identification and diagnostic stages, getting some external support for facilitation and training internal Responsive Professional Learning facilitation experts.

Case study 2 – 'gifting' flexible time

In Model Primary School, where there are five statutory In-Service Training days, one of these days was timetabled at the start of the summer holidays. Another was timetabled at the start of the Christmas holidays, 'gifting' this time for staff to use. In return, staff members were asked to work independently, at a time that suits them throughout the year. This included collaborative time after school, independent study or engaging in reflective practice using videos recorded in lesson time. Staff were encouraged to engage in some kind of Responsive Professional Learning in this time and to spread it fairly evenly across the year.

In addition, there were optional regular 'Tweak of the week' meetings, where staff could share ideas. There were also key stage meetings twice every half term, where staff could collaboratively plan and discuss key ideas.

Comments   This structure provides a great deal of flexibility and independence for staff. They will be free to collaborate with colleagues at a time that suits them, and they can engage in personal study and research. For staff who are quite proactive, this independence is probably very much appreciated.

However, extra time in the holidays does not actually reduce the amount that needs to be completed during term time. There is not anything that is necessarily taken *off* staff's plates during busy term time. This means that this way of structuring professional learning time risks wellbeing with high workload and, therefore, potentially limits how effective any professional learning will be. In addition, it is very unstructured for staff who need guidance and clarity around how best to engage in professional learning. There is a risk that this time is wasted by some staff who are not used to directing their own learning time in a structured way.

Our advice to Model Primary School was to drastically slash the amount of marking, planning and data entry required of teachers to give more time back outside of the two 'gifted days' and to allocate the time from those days in a more structured way. This gives better work-life balance and teachers more space to engage with professional learning.

We suggested that the 'Tweak of the week' be themed to a whole school priority (e.g. literacy) and staff had to present some simple 'before' and 'after' student work examples along with an optional clip of video of a technique in action.

Case study 3 – half-termly cycles

In Illustration Primary, there are half-termly meetings timetabled after school to enable Responsive Professional Learning. Staff choose a key theme and at each meeting they discuss a key element of research that relates to their theme, plan together and then between meetings they are expected to experiment and evaluate their practice. At the next meeting they share their progress. They are encouraged to collaborate in between sessions but there is no additional time provided for this.

In addition, there are phase meetings every half term, weekly provision for new and early career teachers (although all staff are welcome to attend), as well as optional bespoke coaching.

Comments This is a model that we've seen used in a number of schools. It can be a good first step to finding time for Responsive Professional Learning. However, we see a few pitfalls. First, staff need to ensure that they select a theme that is pertinent to their students' needs and which will have strong impact. Sometimes they need support or expert challenge in identifying this. There is a risk staff choosing based on interest or with insufficient depth.

Second, this model includes no time for engagement in between half termly sessions. Many staff forget what they've done from one session to the next and there is a lack of urgency to implement with some staff barely engaging at all through the year. This is exacerbated if they have chosen a theme that is not sufficiently closely linked to their students' needs. There is a risk that staff turn up and have interesting discussions every half term but there is not enough momentum and engagement for this to significantly alter their practice. This is a greater risk when groups are larger.

A third risk is that there is no structured engagement with evidence or research. Who is quality assuring the quality of expertise? Who is challenging assumptions or helping to translate the best ideas from the system into a usable form for the teachers?

Our recommendations to Illustration Primary included using more regular, shorter meetings to keep the momentum going, along with finding ways for students to finish school a little earlier on one day to give staff time. We also suggested that some staff be training in a more formal Responsive Professional Learning such as Lesson Study so that they could bring some of the discipline around diagnostics, evidence and implementation into the whole school processes.

Case study 4 – twilights

In Representative College, two statutory In-Service Training days have been reallocated as eight ninety-minute twilight (after-school) sessions over the year. Based on a staff survey of interests, staff have been grouped into key focus areas, and they are expected to engage in collaborative Responsive Professional Learning based on a key theme. There are mentors who support each group to consider the stages of the cycle – identify, check, explore, do and reflect.

The remaining In-Service days are used for subject-specific planning and engagement with external experts. Some teachers visited other schools, and some experts came in to work with relevant groups.

Comments   Regular twilights should allow staff to engage in sustained and iterative Responsive Professional Learning. This is an effective way of providing time for this time of learning. Just as with half-termly cycles, there should be support for staff to select a pertinent focus that will benefit them and their students.

However, twilights after school can be a difficult time. Part-time staff or staff with other commitments may find it inconvenient or impossible to arrange. In addition, often by the end of the day many staff will be tired and not at their most productive or engaged. As with the previous model, the time gap between sessions may be too long to sustain momentum.

The end of the day can commonly be taken over by parents, detentions or last-minute meetings. It is important that all staff (including leaders) are able to take part in this time.

Teachers also need plenty of time to catch up with administrative tasks. Taking away full In-Service Training days can mean a lack of time to catch up with planning and marking, unless the school has made great strides in reducing overall workload-fuelling demands in these areas.

Our recommendation to Representative College was to use some regular department meeting time for professional learning, as well as less frequent twilights. We suggested that not all staff needed to meet at the same times to give flexibility, and that any whole staff inputs could be videoed and uploaded to let other staff see them later.

Case study 5 – using subject time

At Exampleton High School, most professional learning time has been given over to subject time. Aside from optional coaching, provision for early career teachers and key whole staff In-Service days, professional learning time is all spent in subjects. There are regular meetings, where subject teams collaboratively plan, experiment and evaluate, focused on key areas of the curriculum where there are learning needs. This means all staff are engaged in subject-specific Responsive Professional Learning.

Comments   Effective professional learning needs to be contextualised and should be linked to subject-specific practice. By providing so much subject-specific time, staff will have the opportunity to engage in Responsive Professional Learning focused on curriculum needs and the learning of their students.

However, for a small proportion of staff, this might not be the most effective structure. For example, for some staff it may be more appropriate to focus on behavioural or attitudinal student needs. Other staff teach across multiple subjects while others are part-time and can't make the regular meetings. There can be context specific learning that is not necessarily always linked to subjects. Models where there is some more room for flexibility for staff to collaborate across subjects if relevant can be more powerful.

We were enthusiastic about Exampleton High adopting this model but suggested that they could use some web-based collaboration tools to ensure that staff who couldn't attend a meeting were able to see what had happened. We also suggested that the school used some of its whole-school training days to ensure that cross-curricular links could be made, and aspects of more generic pedagogy explored.

Case study 6 – re-structuring of the school day

At Illustrative Primary School, they have changed the length of school day so that every two weeks, children leave two hours earlier and staff have two hours of professional learning time. Every half term, two of these will be spent in subject teams, one will be spent flexibly (teachers often visit other schools, engage with external experts or engage in personal research), and the remaining three or four will be spent collaborating in triads in Responsive Professional Learning.

In addition, there are In-Service Training days where key school priorities are address, where there is any whole school communication and, sometimes, there is collaboration with other schools.

Comments   This is an excellent model for structuring professional learning as there are regular opportunities to engage in Responsive Professional Learning, as well as to contextualise any learning to subjects. However, this is not always feasible and can be very difficult for schools to arrange. In addition, we have seen some examples where this prompts complacency and some of this time is eaten into for administrative tasks. It is vital that this time is actively preserved for powerful professional learning.

Maintaining the plan

'The best-laid schemes of mice and men often go awry'

There is no such thing as the perfect plan and delivery. We would recommend that senior leaders monitor staff satisfaction throughout the year and adapt their plans where necessary. To increase buy-in, some schools set up a small working group of a range of different types of staff who meet to review feedback from individual activities, reflect on any anecdotal information, gather survey information and review any feedback coming through line management meetings. In the most successful schools we visit, staff members repeatedly tell us how senior leaders 'really listen to our feedback'. To support this, the review group can publicise findings from their research, allowing senior leaders to acknowledge what has been heard and what will be done.

During any year, new priorities and urgent needs will inevitably crop up. Hopefully, these can be dealt with using some of the pre-planned 'flex' slots. If not, then it is helpful to be clear to affected staff about what will be removed in order to make room for the new priority, and why it is being prioritised.

Key ideas

- In addition to collating student needs, consider the needs of individuals, teams and the whole school.
- For each group, consider what will **directly** support improved impact with students, parents and community, and what is intended to **indirectly** do so, through building individual and organisational capacity, leadership and effectiveness.
- For each need, identify the depth of expertise needed and use that to plan an appropriate length of programme.

- Identify all your school's professional learning times and create an annual plan where there is some room to accommodate urgent changes.
- Use a staff working group to monitor feedback during the year.

Middle leadership and professional learning

Middle leadership is often said to be 'the engine room of a school'. Middle leaders provide the key bridge between staff working at the organisational edge and the leadership in the centre of the organisation. As such, they play a key role in collating and communicating the needs at the edge so that they feed into the support and structures available.

Middle leaders of particular phases or subjects are often a source of professional learning for staff. In particular, where schools have reduced budgets or are more focused on developing internal and sustained learning processes, many middle leaders in England play a larger role in professional learning than they did ten years ago.

As such, there needs to be careful consideration of the role that middle leaders play in professional learning, and how they are supported to excel in this role.

The link between the edge and the centre

Too often, we see schools where decisions are made by leaders at the organisational centre and middle leaders and teachers are seen only as mechanisms for delivering these decisions. This can lead to a mismatch, where staff at the edge are well placed to identify needs yet have no opportunity to share these perspectives.

The most successful schools empower their middle leaders to gather perspectives from staff and identify individual and team priorities which then feed into whole school priorities. Team leaders have a level of autonomy so that they can plan and act on particular team needs.

Key roles for middle leaders include:

- Helping their team members identify their own development needs and the particular needs of their students.
- Collating feedback and data to identify team needs or particular areas of the curriculum that need focus.
- Communicating these needs to inform wider school plans.
- Delivering or enabling professional learning that will meet these needs which are specific to the team.

Team leaders should ensure that all their staff are engaged in Responsive Professional Learning. A key part of collaborative time should then be focused on sharing the reflections and evaluations of staff's learning. This, alongside regular developmental conversations, allows team leaders to identify and collate a picture of team needs.

Delivering and enabling professional learning

As team leaders who deliver and enable professional learning, there are a number of key factors for leaders to consider.

Using meeting time

Schools are increasingly spending professional time in departments and teams. Teachers are always pushed for time, so any time spent in departments needs to be used effectively. We've heard from many teachers that meeting time has been dominated by 'housekeeping' and admin. It is easy to spend time sharing information, with little direct benefit to students.

In teams where this professional learning time is working best, meetings are used for high-quality conversations about curriculum, assessment, teaching and learning. Time spent on administration, briefing and monitoring activities is radically reduced, for example through better use of email and online resources, rather than time in person. Colleagues are encouraged to bring specific examples of work (e.g. class work, tests, homework and video clips of performances or interviews with pupils) and these are compared and discussed, with ideas shared about how they might link to prior, current and future curriculum aims. Teachers often work alongside teaching assistants to share teaching strategies as well as the most common ways that students struggle, enabling the whole team to learn and develop together.

In one school we visited, every meeting is kicked off with a fairly challenging exam question. Every teacher has a go and tries to annotate where they feel that students go wrong and what the most impressive answer would be. This is a great way to share ideas, explore pupil misconceptions, build subject knowledge and initiate a conversation about teaching strategies.

Expert input

As discussed in detail in Chapter Five, expert input is a crucial part of effective professional learning. This is often delivered or facilitated within teams, particularly where there are subject specific needs. Many teams invest in linking key teachers with subject associations. They can then forward updates, articles and ideas and share thinking from the association or from a local subject network. This works well at both primary and secondary level. This also enables a more collective view of expertise – it breaks away from the convention that the most senior manager in a team is assumed to have the greatest competence and expertise.

Research is often shared and discussed at team level. This might be through a key role within the department, through engagement with subject associations, newsletters, summaries of research or carefully selected books and blogs.

Where groups of schools collaborate, joint team meetings can also be an opportunity for discussing pedagogy, sharing ideas and practice, and gaining some external perspective and expertise. This can be particularly important for smaller teams or subject areas, where learning from other organisations and contexts can be very powerful.

Building a learning culture within a team or project

Chapter Four explores the importance of culture in professional learning in general. Yet, sometimes within a team you don't necessarily have the opportunity to influence the culture of the whole organisation. It is equally important to build a positive learning culture around a group, team or project. This can be challenging in a toxic wider environment but is something that should be considered and planned for when leading a team or project.

Shared sense of purpose

Relevance and purpose are something to consider carefully when building a learning culture across a group. If the wider culture is not developmental, then it is important to build that shared purpose and the shared learning journey within the team.

- Regularly review the team's ultimate goals – what would success look like for students? What would they go on to do? How would they feel about your team's lessons? How close is the team to producing those outcomes?
- Spend regular time looking at the curriculum. Identify which students you hope to benefit from any learning (if it is focused on students' outcomes) and clarify what would it look like if successful.
- Try to identify what level of experience and expertise colleagues have around each concept and idea. If they have no preconceptions and are new to the concepts being discussed, then clear models and structures are important. If they already have some expertise, then learning something new or developing their understanding and practice will look different (see our second chapter).

If you can get some shared consensus on what success would look like, this not only allows people to buy into the culture and link it back to their own work, but it also means that any learning is much more likely to impact directly on pupils.

Build relationships

Trust and relationships are just as important in a small group. This includes ensuring that colleagues are listened to, that all contributions are valued, and that there is an opportunity for all staff to contribute.

- Encourage open discussion and feedback, show that colleagues are listened to. Use coaching conversations to make sure that everyone is being heard. Ensure that nobody dominates the discussion.
- Celebrate things that do work, but also the learning from where things didn't work. This builds a culture where it's okay to be vulnerable and learn.
- Middle leaders should talk about their own learning to demonstrate that this is a learning team.

Preserve time and space

Particularly if you are building a positive learning culture within a wider school culture that might be a bit more negative, it is important to separate your group's learning and culture from the wider organisation. There are a few things that might help:

- Find a space where you are unlikely to be interrupted. You might even find it helpful to meet somewhere outside of school, although this might risk eating into colleagues' free time.
- Make sure that time is preserved for collaboration and that that time doesn't get eaten into by other things. Model punctuality and how you are prioritising that time. Don't allow one or two team members' lack of punctuality or engagement to become 'the elephant in the room' – address it.

Checklist for middle leaders

- ☐ I play a key role in supporting staff to identify student needs and then collating these to identify team needs.
- ☐ My team meetings are focused on how our practice can be developed to meet student needs.
- ☐ I support my team to engage with expertise and research specific to our team needs.

☐ Colleagues in my team feel encouraged to innovate and contribute to the team's development.

☐ I model and share my own professional learning.

Supporting new and early career teachers

Every great school invests in preparing and nurturing the next generation of educators. This is a specialist area that could take a whole book in itself, so we focus here on some general principles and ideas to help you create adequate provision for new and early career teachers.

New but not new

While student teachers are often new to the teaching profession, they are rarely new to the experience of being in a classroom. There are some aspects of practice and thinking in which they are truly novice while in other areas they already have strongly established mental schema and preconceptions, constructed from their time in the classroom as students.

The education of student teachers is therefore more than helping them acquire the knowledge and skill to carry out new tasks. It requires a move from a potentially idealistic and naïve stance, where explanations are based on their own experience as a school student. It requires the development of sufficient concrete experiences, theories of learning and teaching practices such that these are gradually replaced or deepened by reference to experience from the teacher perspective.

Designing student teachers' learning is complex as you are dealing with people who can be both overwhelmed, struggling novices *and* relatively intransigent, experienced thinkers – all at the same time. It is often an emotional process as it deeply challenges the student teacher's self-perception - their sense of confidence, agency and idealism. Their mental biases mean that they are drawn to filter and interpret what they see and hear through the lens of their existing thinking and values rather than change their thinking in the light of what they see and hear.

An integrated approach

This tension of 'new but not new' has a number of implications for trainee teachers' professional learning. As discussed in Chapter One, learning for novices is best pursued with lots of structure, modelling and the breaking down of complex tasks into smaller ones with practice, repetition and feedback. It is built up gradually to allow the novice to achieve a balance of confidence-building success and skill-building constructive failure.

Learning for those with more expertise or existing mental models needs more experimentation. It is carefully designed to help them see new perspectives which are in conflict with existing mental models in order to change and enhance these. It requires external support and challenge with a coaching stance to help make existing thinking explicit, constructively challenge it and attend to the emotional and self-perception elements.

Example: planning a lesson

New teachers take longer to plan teaching and learning as they need to carefully envision the lesson they are about to deliver – they go into greater detail, familiarise themselves with ideas and resources and spend longer reviewing plans with others.

From the novice stance, lesson planning involves preparing for activities and processes which are unfamiliar. As Kennedy[1] would put it, they are preparing to pursue six concurrent priorities:

a. deliver/model/explain the required content;
b. facilitate and monitor the learning of that content;
c. monitor and increase students' engagement;
d. maintain lesson momentum/keep to time;
e. develop a civil classroom community; and
f. regulate their own emotional state.

In addition, they bring their existing schema and mental models. Student teachers are more likely to confuse and conflate some of these aspects due to their own school experience. They are likely to focus initially on simple delivery of material and the more obvious approaches to behaviour management. These are the elements that will have been most visible when they were students.

They are likely to be less aware of how their own learning was facilitated, how formative assessment was sought or the subtler approaches to creating a positive, civil and well-ordered classroom environment.

To support the development of these student teachers, they will need guided support in preparing the lesson, they might benefit from role-play around managing transitions, and clear prepared strategies for behaviour will support them. But in addition, they need to engage in more sustained learning around what makes a good scheme of learning, developing deliberative practice around how a curriculum is sequenced. They will also need to experiment and refine their delivery through support from a mentor, who can help them develop adaptive expertise, responding to the needs of the classroom.

Key content for new and early career teachers

The best programmes for beginning teachers that we have seen tend to include:

■ In-depth exploration of 'schemes of learning', showing how concepts, knowledge, skills are developed over a longer period of time and how this fits into the wider curriculum sequencing. Individual lessons should be understood as part of a wider scheme of learning. It can be helpful to reflect on a range of samples of work from previous students that help to explore different levels of understanding and success in the lesson.

■ Individual activities and key transitions are prepared and practised in advance – watching and reflecting as other teachers carry them out. Micro-teaching can be a useful activity – trying out simple procedures in front of the mentor or peers or even taking a few minutes of another teacher's lesson to try small lesson elements. This is more important earlier on in the student teacher's experience.

■ Careful consideration and support for managing behaviour. Fear of managing behaviour can rapidly overwhelm all other considerations without sufficient support. It can be very helpful to pre-prepare a number of proactive and reactive strategies, to micro-teach them, as well as help the student teacher see them in action from more experienced practitioners.

- Guided observations and reflections – opportunities to engage in carefully designed observations **of** other teachers and **by** other teachers. Ideally these need:
  - time beforehand to carefully plan what will be looked for and how to look for it;
  - carefully designed observation templates to structure and focus what is being looked at; and
  - individual or group reflection and feedback with minimal delay after the observation. This can be supported if the lesson has also been captured on video. The facilitator needs a high level of expertise to get the right balance of support and challenge.
- Support with lesson content – regular and in-depth development of understanding of what it is being taught, how students learn it, how best to teach and assess it. Even though student teachers may have a general mastery of a topic then there is a need to deal with the 'curse of knowledge' – the inability to remember what it is like to not know or understand something. Therefore, support around content should always be integrated with support around how to model skills or explain ideas, what challenges or misconceptions are common, great tasks and questions to use to formatively assess, and a broader understanding of why the curriculum has been carefully designed to build long-term learning. Where possible, support around content should be given as close as possible to the time where student teachers need to apply it in their classroom.

Case study

Student teachers at Greyich Academy receive dedicated, weekly training sessions from experienced initial teacher educators. They also engage in whole-school staff development sessions. Early on in the year, the sessions for student teachers focus on the real basics – behaviour management, key classroom transitions, and some fundamentals in lesson planning and marking. The group uses video clips of effective lessons and members engage in some simple role-playing to practise and refine techniques. There can also be elements of problem-solving – bringing issues that have cropped up to discuss and share. As the student teachers become more experienced, the support becomes more responsive to the collective needs of the group, addressing issues that are cropping up.

In addition, subject mentors work alongside the student teacher to support subject knowledge and how to plan, teach and assess different topics. These mentors collaborate and supervise in lessons to give regular feedback.

Every student teacher has a link to a university where they are able to work with an academic mentor to help them access and make links to educational research and theory. All the mentors, both in-school and university-based, recognise each other's strengths and have carefully mapped and planned their support to be complementary.

Student teachers are also invited to most whole staff training sessions which helps make them part of the staff team, learn about institutional norms and contribute to discussions.

Commentary

This example is taken from a school where student teachers told us that felt very well supported. They have access to guided practice, as well as to learning that is responsive to their needs. They also have access to subject expertise and evidence-informed strategies.

Our only suggestion was that the school could add in some one-to-one coaching and mentoring sessions with each student teacher, where they explicitly check assumptions that are being made and provide individual support at a very challenging time.

Support staff and professional learning

'Support staff' refers to all staff in schools who are not employed as teachers. This does not mean that they don't work with children or contribute to their development, but includes a wide-range of roles. Whilst *support staff* is not an unproblematic term, as these colleagues not only support teachers but are vital to the running of an effective school, it is the most commonly used term and one we use here.

As we outlined in the introduction, when we refer to 'teachers' in this book this is shorthand for *educators and staff that work with students*. Similarly, this book focuses on professional learning for both direct and indirect impact. This means that most of our content can be applied to support staff, too. However, in this section we explore this further.

In our work with schools, we see that professional learning for support staff in most cases lags behind what is available for teaching staff. It is not uncommon to see:

- Very little professional learning available for support staff. Some have no clear performance management processes and experience very little training beyond that required for their statutory duties.
- Support staff who are expected to attend the same training as teachers, some of which is irrelevant and therefore frustrating.
- The bulk of professional learning being one-off and out-of-school. Expert input is crucial for effective professional learning, but it is not cost-effective or likely to have an impact if it is occurring in isolation and is not part of a wider programme.
- A lack of career development or seeing the role and development of teaching assistants solely as a route to teacher training, rather than a skilled role in itself with options to transition into other roles.

Of course, there are major differences when considering the professional learning of non-teaching staff compared to teaching staff. These differences often come with real challenges, some of which are listed below:

- Non-teaching staff are likely to be on different contracts which make finding time for professional learning more difficult, or in addition to salary costs.
- Many non-teaching staff will be the only person in their role, so opportunities for collaboration are different – they may not be able to leave their post to work with others. This is a particularly acute role for front-of-house roles, e.g. those on reception or answering phones.
- There are fewer established routes for career progression for many non-teaching roles.
- Many schools have a history of not prioritising or managing professional learning for support staff, which has set different expectations and a different starting point to non-teaching staff.
- Some support staff may not have qualifications to such a high level and may need support to engage in academic study to open doors for future career moves.

Yet, despite these challenges, there are many examples of schools with excellent practice. Here, we outline some key principles to consider when planning professional learning for support staff. It is split into two halves – professional learning for support staff who work directly with children and professional learning for support staff who don't.

Professional learning for support staff who work directly with children

Professional learning for support staff who work directly with children – such as teaching assistants, pastoral workers and some technicians – shares similar key principles to professional learning for teaching staff. In fact, in many cases, it is appropriate for support staff to collaborate with teaching colleagues.

Cultivate a culture of learning

Even the most effective professional learning processes are dependent on a positive learning culture. Just as it is important to build a developmental culture for teachers, it is important to cultivate a belief that professional learning is valued for all staff. All staff should feel safe to carefully experiment and try new things out, and should feel valued as professionals.

One key change schools can make is to ensure that they consider and include support staff in briefings and look for opportunities to build a truly integrated collegiate team. Don't segregate your staff, but also don't expect people to sit through things that are largely irrelevant to their role.

It is also important to support collaboration, peer observation, collaborative planning and the sharing of practice amongst all staff. Too often, meeting time and collaborative time is provided for teachers in a way that it isn't for non-teaching staff. Non-teaching staff may need trained deputies or to have colleagues who can comfortably cover for them.

Finally, make sure that professional learning is prioritised, resourced and celebrated. This might include providing time, preserving a space for collaboration, supporting opportunities for accreditation and expert input, and just talking about and modelling professional learning.

Do

- Do make sure that you build a collegiate culture where all staff take part in whole school meetings, events and feed into key decisions.
- Do build teams and leaders amongst support staff and empower them to have as much influence and recognition as teams of teachers have.

Don't

- Don't make staff sit through things that are irrelevant to them – be mindful of whole staff time being relevant to all.
- Don't forget that that support staff will benefit from collaboration and meeting time in the same way as teachers should.

Ensure professional learning is driven by and linked to student needs

Support staff who work with students will have professional learning that is *directly* linked to students, parents and community, as well as some learning that *indirectly* supports this. There should be careful planning of how both of these are met through professional learning. It is not uncommon for professional learning for support staff to be focused on indirect and procedural processes, rather than building adaptive expertise that best supports those that they work with.

This means that support staff who work with children, just like teachers, should engage in identifying student needs and directing their learning accordingly. Throughout any professional learning activity, staff should consider the students who they expect to benefit, and then in their practice they should experiment with new strategies and evaluate whether it has met the expected impact.

This process can be supported through collaborative processes and Responsive Professional Learning. It is vital that support staff who work with children are given the time, space and support to engage in such processes.

Examples

- At Case Study Primary School, all teachers and teaching assistants are involved in 'Learning Hubs'. They are a form of Responsive Professional Learning, where staff meet twice every half term and identify a defined focus, engage with research and try a strategy in pairs within the Hub. Some support staff who are unable to attend sessions after school (they have different contracts to teachers) are able to meet at lunch time, and those who do meet after school are paid accordingly.
- At E G High School, a teaching assistant who worked closely with a number of students for whom English was an additional language (EAL students) was given responsibility for developing school-wide strategies for these students. He visited a number of other schools, attended a local conference and worked with the wider teaching and learning team to support staff across the school.

Do

- Do plan the time, resource and structure for support staff to engage in Responsive Professional Learning processes.
- Do provide the opportunity for support staff and teachers to collaborate when focused on a similar student learning or curriculum issue.

Don't

- Don't forget to consider the culture. Many support staff will be less used to engaging in Responsive Professional Learning opportunities, as sadly there is a history of their learning being less carefully planned.
- Don't forget to consider how any differing timetables or contracts might impact on the opportunity for support staff to engage in such processes.

Engage in the theory and the practical context of your learning

Effective professional learning includes both engaging in the theory and evidence, as well as contextualising and embedding it in your own practice. This can be supported through collaboration with HEIs, direct engagement with research, input from experts, using research summaries or colleagues in school to support the dissemination of research.

We are seeing a renewed drive for evidence-informed schools and many teachers are engaging more deeply with research. This should also be supported amongst non-teaching staff.

Examples

- At X1 School, all learning support assistants engage in teaching and learning communities where each half term they read and discuss a key piece of research, then determine some relevant strategies to experiment with in their work. At the next meeting they then share their evaluations.
- At Exemplar Primary, a teaching assistant and a pastoral worker are engaged in their own further study (one completing a degree and one a Masters). Much of their work and research is feeding into their practice. A member of reception staff is being trained in coaching techniques to work more effectively with parents.

Enable opportunities for expert input

It is hard to learn something new. We are inclined towards sticking to what we know and rejecting what is unfamiliar and what doesn't suit our existing outlook. As such, it is important to engage with external expertise that can disrupt our assumptions. Obviously, experts can also provide evidence-informed input and support, too.

All staff should have access to external input and challenge, including opportunities to visit other schools, access to evidence-informed input, and the opportunity to seek out different approaches and strategies. The National Association of Professional Teaching Assistants, the Teaching Assistant Standards, subject associations, the Specialist SEND Association, and the EEF Teaching Assistant Guidance can all be helpful sources for this in England.

Examples

- A local group of schools regularly collaborate. This includes a regular forum for pastoral staff, who often have relatively few colleagues to collaborate with within school. They meet every half term, but also regularly visit one another's schools to observe different approaches in different contexts.

Do

- Do consider how support staff will access external expertise, from within or outside the school.
- Do plan how this expertise meets specific needs. Often support staff have the most access to external input, but it is often not closely linked to their own or their students' needs.

Don't

- Don't engage with external experts which don't have a strong evidence-base behind their approach.

Professional learning for general support staff

Support staff who do not work with children are sadly often forgotten about in a school's professional learning programme. Yet, many of the principles of effective learning for staff who work with children still apply.

Cultivate a culture of learning

Professional learning for non-teaching staff is often focused on statutory training or career development. While both of these are important, it is also important to prioritise developing and learning within your role. Professional learning is not just about fixing problems but about best meeting school needs and continually working to develop, and this is something that should be shared and celebrated.

This is partly aided by a positive learning culture, by providing time and resource, by enabling collaboration and the sharing of practice, but also by effective line management, which supports and encourages development opportunities.

Examples

■ At Green Middle School, there are carefully planned performance management structures for all staff, with line management for general support staff working across a group of schools, so that they are well supported by staff who have experience in their work. Every new member of support staff also receives a mentor as part of a buddy system so that their induction runs as smoothly as possible.

Do

■ Do model your own learning and explicitly promote how professional learning is part of your school culture.
■ Do celebrate learning and innovation among all staff.

Don't

■ Don't forget to provide opportunities for staff who might be the only ones in their role; allow opportunities for collaboration with other schools and provide appropriate appraisal systems.

Expert input and engaging with theory

All of us need expert challenge to support us to learn. We also all need to ensure we are engaging in evidence-informed practices. As such, it is just as important for non-teaching members of staff to have opportunities to engage with experts as it is for teachers. School visits are perhaps particularly important, as non-teaching staff are even more likely to be the only ones working in their role.

Associations such as the National Association of School Business Management and National Network of School Site Staff can provide this expert input. Similarly, Skills for Schools, a website managed by Unison, provides a number of resources and opportunities in England – http://www.skillsforschools.org.uk/.

Examples

■ A School Business Manager regularly engages with her association and with colleagues at other schools through local forums and social media. This allows her to constantly review and challenge her ways of working, to be up to date on any new approaches, and to build her awareness of possible areas for development.

Do

■ Do provide opportunities to collaborate with other schools and organisations.
■ Do expect engagement with evidence-informed ideas in every area of the school.

Don't

■ Don't expect staff to engage with external expertise with no time and resource to take forward and embed new ideas.

Professional learning is driven by need

Whilst staff who don't work with children might not need to link their learning directly to an expected student outcome, they do need to link it to a clear school need and evaluate how they meet that need. Some needs will be quite specific and procedural, such as completing first aid training or learning how to use the school data programme more effectively. However, there will be more complex skills and knowledge that need to be learned in a sustained and focused way. For example, leading and managing others, reassessing and developing the approach to school events, reviewing and developing how the school tracks all data, or reviewing and developing a school-wide approach to professional learning.

Sadly, it is quite rare to see non-teaching staff given much role in school improvement projects and action research. Yet, when schools have done this, it can result in significant engagement and improvements. It is important that schools deliver powerful professional learning for all staff, enabling not only an improvement in staff motivation and wellbeing, but also in a more efficient and effective school, where students and staff succeed.

Examples

■ One member of office staff at a large secondary school was given the time to research how different organisations approach performance management. With a team of colleagues, she then re-designed how appraisal works to be more in line with evidence-informed approaches.
■ In a primary school, the school receptionist was encouraged, after giving feedback, to re-design how school events worked, which resulted in higher parental attendance and the day went much more smoothly.

Do

- Do ensure that support staff feed into school decision making.
- Do be open to and encourage flexibility and initiative. Support staff work at the edge of the organisation and are well placed to identify possible opportunities and innovations.

Don't

- Don't ignore opportunities for development in role, as well as opportunities for career development.

Effective professional learning enables all staff to best meet their own needs and the needs of their school. The most effective professional learning is responsive and enables staff to be engaged in identifying opportunities and areas for development within the school.

The most successful schools will have a developmental culture where all staff are empowered to develop and innovate, creating success across the organisation. Whilst schools' core purpose is the direct impact they have on students' learning, good processes that indirectly benefit students should not be forgotten and can enable the best opportunities for our children.

Governance and professional learning

A well-functioning organisation enjoys effective governance – strategic guidance and challenge that supports long-term success.

As a leader of professional development, you need a strong working relationship with governors, trustees or board members. In this chapter, we explore governors' own learning, key items for reporting to a board, some key questions which governors should be asking and ideas around the evidence that can be helpful for senior leaders to present to the governing board.

Professional learning for governors

Just as for employed staff, governors need access to their own professional learning. This should include support for developing in the role of governor, as well as access to learning both about the education sector and the particular context and needs of the individual school. This normally involves engaging with expertise both internal and external to the school.

Because of the nature of governors' roles, a much larger proportion of their professional learning will be for building awareness and deliberative expertise. This means that their professional learning will likely entail shorter periods of engagement than when developing adaptive expertise.

There should be a careful analysis of individual board members' needs, balanced with school priorities of which governors need to have a secure understanding.

Reporting to a governing board

Governors need to be well informed of work across the school. Professional learning for staff should be a key priority for governors; they need to ensure that staff have access to it and that it is supporting success for both staff and students.

When reporting, a variety of sources should be used to gather information. Governors should expect information from the senior leadership, but should also make time to examine professional development plans and speak to a variety of staff themselves. It is important to unpick the focus of the professional learning, any needs analysis and impact measurements, as well as the effectiveness of processes used.

It is good practice to have one named governor who is responsible for overseeing the school's approaches to professional development. This governor can arrange conversations and visits to speak to the professional learning leader as well as other staff. It is also helpful to get an external audit of the school's approach and ensure that the school is connected to leading practice in this area.

Above all, school leaders need to provide sufficient information to governors so that they can ask informed, supportively challenging questions. However, governors need to maintain the all-important line of being strategic, not operational, leaving space for leaders to develop their own solutions.

A question checklist

Governors need to get the right information to monitor the professional development programme. Here are some questions to think about, along with a few suggestions of where to seek this information.

- ☐ How much money is being spent on the full variety of professional development activities and programmes? What are the plans to increase this? This goes beyond courses, seminars and sessions and looks at experts brought in, time released for staff, tools and resources procured. *Evidence: budgets, discussion with the bursar/business manager.*
- ☐ How much time is allocated for staff to engage in professional learning? What are the plans to extend this? Is time allocated or released for **all** staff, including non-teaching staff, to engage in professional development and developmental collaboration? *Evidence: staff timetables, discussion with the professional learning leader, conversations with staff.*
- ☐ Do professional development activities have specific pupil outcomes associated with them or is there a general logic model? Is the impact of each activity being evaluated upon these outcomes? *Evidence: school self-evaluation forms, professional learning monitoring documents.*
- ☐ Is the school supporting teaching and professional development with a coherent, expertly designed curriculum along with associated resources and guides? Are assessments and data collected focused primarily on helping teachers, or are they seen as burdensome and top-down? *Evidence: discussions with subject leaders, teachers. Viewing assessment policies and data systems.*
- ☐ What is the programme of professional learning activities for the year? Are individual activities being threaded together into coherent programmes? How long is each professional learning focus being sustained for – are these one-off activities or long-term approaches? *Evidence: school professional learning plans, records of the previous year, conversations with staff.*
- ☐ How is the school ensuring that it is engaging with quality providers? Is it strategically finding and comparing courses and consultancy - e.g. on a national database

(such as TDT Advisor)? *Evidence: professional learning policy, conversations with professional learning leader.*

☐ What steps is the school taking to ensure that up-to-date, evidence-based approaches to teaching are being actively sought and embedded? Is the school engaging with expert organisations? *Evidence: senior leaders, conversations with staff. Evidence of some QA and efforts to engage with a full range of evidence.*

☐ Is every member of staff (including non-teaching staff) being proactively supported in their career development? *Evidence: conversations with staff/surveys.*

☐ Is the school getting support and challenge around the way that it develops professional learning? Is the professional learning role integrated or isolated? How is it developing leadership of staff development? *Evidence: conversation with senior leaders, audit or QA process reports.*

☐ Does every member of staff feel supported and constructively challenged? Do they feel trusted and valued? How are school leaders ensuring that top-down performance management and quality assurance processes aren't hindering a culture of professional learning? *Evidence: conversations with staff, senior leaders.*

Career routes and professional learning

The words 'professional learning' for some people are immediately associated with career development and career progression. That is not the main focus of this book. This is a manifesto for how professional learning and development even within your role can support children to succeed and teachers to thrive. However, effective support for career development is a key part of any successful organisation.

There's a bigger reason too. If teaching is going to draw on the collective expertise of the entire profession, then teachers need opportunity to develop that expertise and be recognised for it. We need much more than just recognition of leadership. We need to develop and accredit expertise in all specialisms and in general classroom practice.

Supporting career development

Whilst much of the focus of this book is on professional learning focused on the organisational edge, it is important to develop the structures in the middle that support development. This is where career development falls, we would argue. Opportunities to progress and develop in one's career is motivating, rewarding, offers challenge, and ultimately builds the skills and roles that are needed in a complex organisation for success.

It would be possible to fill a huge catalogue with the various different career possibilities for teachers in different areas of the world. However, there are some key principles to consider around career development and when planning professional learning, which we have included below.

■ It's much more than just leadership and management.
There are so many aspects of the teaching profession in which one can become an expert. To be an effective institution, schools need to develop expertise in, for example:

■ Subjects
■ Students' phases of development
■ Special Education Needs and Disabilities

- Assessment
- Curriculum Design
- Parental engagement
- Research engagement and evaluation.

If career pathways offered in your school suggest that the only thing valued is management then it sends a powerful, negative signal about the importance of other expertise. We absolutely must stop assuming that the most senior managers must also therefore be the greatest experts in all of the above areas.

- It's bigger than any one institution.

If a school only leaves room for staff to progress for its own benefit, it does a great disservice to the rest of the system. Imagine the power if every school allowed its teachers to flourish as experts in many areas, giving them time to work not only within the institution but also outside of it, with other schools.

In our view, schools must work together in groups to ensure that each cluster has expertise in every subject and specialism. This is particularly urgent and important for smaller schools that will never have the capacity to otherwise develop nor access local expertise in every discipline and domain.

- It needs dedicated time and resource within and across schools.

When timetabling professional learning, it is important to ensure time and space for individuals to reflect upon and discuss their own plans for career development. Without specific time to reflect upon it, career development can fall off the radar, resulting in some staff feeling disempowered and frustrated. Similarly, without specific time to discuss, discussions around career progression can be limited to only the most proactive staff. This risks missing out on potentially very effective colleagues who are less forthcoming, or who are perhaps based on the other side of the school building. It is vital that career progression is something that is transparent and open to all.

To ensure transparency and inclusivity around career development,

- all staff should know who they can approach to discuss their career development;
- there should be allocated time for all staff to discuss it with their line manager; and
- any vacancies should be advertised clearly to all staff.

Similarly, groups of schools can work together to identify times for their cluster to put on specialist training for certain areas – e.g. certain subjects or leadership roles.

- Carefully consider your whole staff body.

Don't forget to consider *all* staff and how they might progress. We often see schools where support staff are largely forgotten in terms of career development. We also see lots of opportunities for teachers to progress into leadership, but not necessarily specific support for developing into pastoral positions of leadership.

This does not mean you have to force staff to progress every year, but you should ensure that all staff are involved in regular conversations around their development and potential career progression, and you should be flexible and open to what career trajectories might look like. For example, a school receptionist in one school we visited, identified some improvements that could be made in a school careers event and was given an opportunity to develop events management into part of her role.

Site staff can progress to lead teams or become experts in specific areas, offering advice to groups of schools. Catering staff can specialise and train to become lead chefs. Teaching assistants can become specialists in niche areas and needs, undergoing study and supporting teachers and other assistants with expertise in these areas.

There should be sufficient flexibility for staff to feed into their own career route. Job shadowing, mentoring, working with other schools can all be invaluable tools in this.

■ Consider the depth of expertise needed.

To illustrate this idea, let's consider management. To become an effective manager, there are a wide range of skills that need to be developed. Some of them are relatively procedural, such as learning the process for recording appraisal conversations. Some are more deliberative, such as creating and managing a budget. Many are adaptive, such as having a line management meeting. When planning professional learning around these skills, careful planning and consideration are needed to match the learning experience to the depth of expertise required. A one-off input is probably sufficient to explain procedural processes in schools, but developing a team will need to be learned over a sustained period, with lots of opportunities for Responsive Professional Learning.

Career routes and professional learning

In addition to supporting career development in general, we want to consider what options teachers have to develop in their career. In many countries, England included, most career progression opportunities for teachers are limited to less time in the classroom and more time managing and leading. There isn't yet a clear role or route to become an 'expert teacher'.

In contrast, in Singapore teachers can choose to develop into senior, lead and master teachers; into leadership (including system leadership); and into particular specialist roles. This recognises the different skills required to fulfil all these roles in schools and rightly celebrates and rewards the teacher who has developed significant expertise.

We call for all systems to reflect similar models, where highly developed and skilled teaching is recognised in a career framework. Not only that, but where particular specialisms, including the skills needed to develop other teachers, are specifically developed and recognised.

Delivering expertise

At some point, every teacher needs to present their ideas to others. While we've spent the whole book arguing against a diet consisting only of one-size-fits-nobody lectures, we felt that it's useful to present a few ideas about how to make *any* presentation that little bit better.

Designing presentations

The majority of training sessions will use a deck of slides to support the learning experience. The design and delivery of these slides is a crucial factor in effective teacher learning. Done well, these slides can simplify and support the learning process. Done wrong, they can confuse, complicate and demotivate.

One of my greatest fears is the presenter who spends an hour reading out dense slides of text, one after the other, in a dull monotone. We wouldn't accept that sort of delivery from a teacher in a classroom, so why should we put up with it for training professionals?
(Quote from a teacher we worked with)

Fortunately, a lot is known about effective presentations. There have been a number of experiments conducted using variations of slides which have shown that simple changes in design can make a huge difference in the amount that participants learn.

Applying cognitive science to slide design

The ideas about how our brains learn that we discussed in Chapter One help us design better slides. For better learning experiences we need to:

- Restrict the number of ideas presented such that participants never have more than three to five chunks of information to work on at any time.
- Design slides to encourage activation of both sound and image working memory at the same time, in complementary ways – this can be done well with a simple image on screen while the presenter talks about it.
- Avoid unhelpful distractions which take up valuable chunks of working memory – both on the slides and in the room – fewer distracting graphics and design features.

Slide design

If you rush to design slides for training, it is easy to write down prompts for speaking as the text, and then read them aloud. However, this is damaging to participants' learning.

1. We naturally read at our own rate – this will be slightly different for each person and depends on reading ability and familiarity with the content.
2. If left to read, each person in the room will be processing a slightly different part of the text on a slide at any moment in time.
3. However, if a presenter is reading the words out loud then every participant must force their attention to the word currently being read – either jumping forwards or holding back. This constantly interrupts the natural rate of processing and makes it impossible to linger on hard-to-understand text or accelerate through familiar ideas.
4. Alternatively, they may try and ignore the presenter, focusing effort on trying to filter out the extra sounds they are hearing.
5. The overall impact is that every participant in the room finds the process:
   a. Uncomfortable – they are less in control of what is happening.
   b. Taxing – they must expend energy and memory to keep monitoring the narrator and pushing their attention in the right place.
   c. Less easy to understand – all that effort and lack of control means that lots of the working memory is taken up just keeping up.

Conclusion: Rule number one of slides –
don't read out the text.

A better approach

There have been a number of experiments to show that good slide design can actively increase learning. Here is a summary of key ideas.

- Use highly simplified diagrams or highly relevant visuals where possible. If combined with simple audio explanation, then this can take advantage of the way that we process learning.

- Avoid lots of distracting design – logos, page numbers, visual flourishes make a slide look appealing but can seriously distract from the important content. This is especially true when presenting information that is less familiar. In particular:
  - Avoid using more than three colours and bear in mind that most audiences include someone who is red-green colour blind, and many have completely colour-blind participants.
  - Avoid using too many font styles (including use of colours, bold, underline, size) – aim for no more than three on a slide. Use simple fonts which work on most computers – Helvetica or Arial are good choices.
  - Use animation very sparingly – it can easily be more distracting than helpful.
  - Use lines and boxes sparingly – boxes around objects and lots of underlines can reduce the impact overall. The best lines are used to separate ideas or link ideas.
  - Use high-contrast colours/text and keep font sizes readable by someone in the back with poor eyesight. You should never have to say 'I know this is probably too small to read, but…' – this is just lazy design.
- Label diagrams or graphs carefully – put the label as close as possible to the element it refers to. Avoid making the viewer follow long lines to the labels or having to jump from numbered visuals to a table of descriptions. This wastes valuable attention and working memory.
- Keep explanatory text very short and precise. Participants will be mentally combining this with visuals and what they are currently hearing.
- Consider not reading out large chunks of text – allow the audience to read it at their own pace. Alternatively, present a relevant visual and read the text instead.
- Don't overload slides – each one should represent a key idea with no more than a small handful of concepts which can be combined together. Even putting two separate ideas on one slide means that some participants will be distracted by the other point at the critical moment of learning.
- Don't overload participants – avoid introducing too many new ideas all in one go. Give opportunities for exploring and questioning and allow participants to take regular breaks to refresh their concentration.
- Use concrete examples and comparisons where possible, instead of using only theoretical and abstract ideas. Worked examples of new ideas are particularly helpful when the ideas are fairly new or unfamiliar to most people. However, for participants who are already expert these may be slightly at odds with existing ideas and could impede learning.

The key to effective slide design is editing. While you may begin by dumping all your ideas on to the slide deck, you should repeatedly go through and:

1. Simplify each slide, removing distractions and separating multiple ideas.
2. Use the dual power of *image* and *sound* memory to move key ideas to narrator notes.
3. Aim to deliver less information but engage participants more deeply in it, in multiple ways.

Effective delivery

The presenter's brain works the same way as the learner's brain. You want to keep your working memory as free as possible to process and respond to the audience. The more you have to focus on absorbing your content, the worse you will be as a presenter. Here are a few key things to think about.

Automaticity

If you are very familiar with a slide, then it takes up much less working memory. Where an unfamiliar slide deck will require the presenter to focus most of their working memory on working out what to do on each slide, a familiar slide can be recalled quickly and efficiently. This leaves plenty of room in working memory for you to:

- Monitor your own delivery and state.
- Keep a constant check on timings and progress.
- Monitor the room for understanding or issues.
- Make decisions to amend your delivery.

If you are delivering an important presentation which needs to have high impact, then you want to be as familiar as possible with the content.

> *We have a few set piece training events in our school during every year. I know that I may be using up to an hour of each staff member's time. Our school is large so this could be one hundred hours of staff time used up in one session. We made the decision that we would set aside time for the presenter to have two practice runs with one or two people to watch and critique, as well as video to watch back with a coach. By investing a few hours of staff time beforehand, we massively improve the quality of the main training event. The presenter felt much more confident and staff were happy that we respected their time and professionalism.*
>
> *(Quote from a headteacher)*

Effective verbal delivery

A great speaker can hold us spellbound. Time slips away as we hang on every word, feel immersed in every story and feel lifted by great wisdom. We don't just listen, we watch as they capture the whole stage.

On the other hand, we've all sat through spectacularly boring presenters. Lacking energy and enthusiasm, they drone out words in a monotone. No matter how much attention we exert, it's hard to listen and even harder to learn. We get lost in over-complex sentences and feel punch-drunk from a barrage of complex, technical vocabulary.

Some elements of speaking

- **Pitch** – how high or low your voice is on average. Men tend to have a lower pitch and women tend to have a higher pitch. The pitch of your voice usually gets higher when you are stressed or surprised. To sound relaxed, it can be helpful to aim for a *slightly* lower pitch than normal conversation, but don't get too self-conscious about this.
- **Intonation** – how your voice rises and falls. To get a sense, read the phrase 'you like it' and now compare to the question 'you like it?' which goes up at the end. Clear intonation helps the audience to understand your meaning. Flat intonation is both confusing and boring to listen to.
- **Tone** – the character of your voice. This is often related to how you use your muscles and how you are breathing. Tense throat muscles and shallow breathing can

lead to a tight or nasal-sounding voice. More relaxed muscles – usually with better posture – and breathing from the diaphragm help your voice sound more relaxed. This makes you easier to listen to.

■ **Pace**. The speed at which you deliver your words. A normal conversation might be 160 to 200 words per minute. Winston Churchill trained himself to speak at around 125 words per minute, while a sports commentator might speak at over 250 words per minute. For larger audiences, slower pace is helpful.

■ **Articulation** or **diction**. The clarity of your pronunciation. Slurring words or missing syllables and sounds makes you harder to understand. The best speakers sound crisp and clear, though this isn't the same as pretending to 'be posh'.

■ **Emphasis**. Meaning can be changed by emphasising different words. For example, if you take the phrase 'I like potatoes' then we could either say 'I *like* potatoes' (to emphasise the liking, perhaps to contrast with someone else not liking them) or 'I like *potatoes*' (to emphasise that it is potatoes you like, not some other type of food). You are combining intonation and pace to produce this emphasis.

Make an impression

If someone walks in for an interview, you make an instant judgement about them based on the way they dress, the way they hold themselves, the way they look at you. Your voice makes a similar impression. The presenter's first words set the scene, they create or prevent rapport. This table suggests some issues to avoid.

Speaking trait	Audience judgement
Too loud/forceful	*Arrogant*
Too quiet, volume fades	*Shy, indecisive, low self-esteem*
Too fast, stumbling over words	*Nervy, anxious*
Too slow, monotone	*Boring, lacking empathy*
Nasal, rising intonation, shrill	*Complainer, lacking authority*
Slurring words, dropping syllables	*Lazy, careless, not clever*

Why not video yourself speaking and watch a two-minute section back to identify which areas you can improve on?

It's worth avoiding a few key 'presentation crimes':

■ Apologising at the start of your talk. This could be 'sorry, I always go on' or 'sorry, I don't really know that much more about this than you do'. You might think you're being humble, but the audience feels insulted and resentful at both.

■ Failing to keep to time. Whatever you do, be clear on when you should finish and learn how to finish with a few minutes to spare. Nothing irritates participants and organisers more than people who can't keep to time.

The appropriate delivery will depend on the audience and venue. Conversational speech – generally flatter and less varied in delivery – is more appropriate for smaller groups. We expect a change of delivery once the group gets bigger; typically, around six or more people requires a more presentational and less conversational tone. The larger the audience grows, the more energy, colour and contrast we need to bring to our voice.

Here are some tips for your voice when speaking to larger audiences.

1. Speak slower but vary your pace. Nerves make some people rush while others turn into robots. 140 words per minute is a good rate to aim for.
2. Increase emphasis on key words and phrases. When presenting, you need to make it as easy as possible for others to follow you. The audience will find you easier to understand if you emphasise the most important points by introducing slight pauses after them. It's a good idea to aim for short pauses around every seven to nine words, with longer pauses after a few sentences. Pauses also help you to reduce 'umms', 'ahhs' and 'errs' in your speaking.
3. Keep your shoulders and throat relaxed. If you notice yourself getting tense, pause for a deep breath, exhaling slower than normal, allowing your shoulders to drop. Practise doing this at home and feel the relaxed, open feeling in your throat when you have breathed deeply and then said 'Ahhhhhhh' in a fairly low pitch. This is the feeling you want to aim for at all times when speaking.

Body language, gesture, facial expression

You probably know the famous song lyric, '*it ain't what you say, it's the way that you say it*'. I'd probably change this to '*it **is** what you say **and** the way that you say it – that's what gets results*'.

When a presenter is speaking, the audience are not only listening to them but also watching. All of the information is being combined together to try and form meaning. The presenter's body and facial movements can either enhance this process or they can hinder it. A presenter needs to consider:

a. Is your body readable – are your gestures, expressions and movements clear and easy to see without being overly exaggerated?
b. Are your movements well aligned with the meaning you are trying to convey?

Anxiety

It is entirely normal to feel nervous when presenting. We are acutely aware that we are about to put ourselves in front of a large number of peers and they will be making judgements about us. However, for some people the idea of public speaking or presenting creates fear that is debilitating.

There are a few key strategies to help – some are short term and others work over longer periods of time.

Prepare

1. **Breathing exercises**. As soon as you begin to feel nervous, focus on taking slow, deep breaths and gradually allow your muscles to relax. You may want to stretch – the same way you would before bed – and/or shake your body, arms and legs to loosen muscles.
2. **Practise**. Find somewhere alone to practise your presentation out loud – the ideal is the same venue that you will use on the day. If you have a particularly important presentation, then find an opportunity to give the same presentation to a smaller

group before-hand. Some of the top TED talk speakers practise their presentations over fifty times before the big day.

Deliver

3. **Keep breathing**. Ensure you are putting in enough pauses and give yourself time to take a sip of water and take a quiet deep breath. Use the moment to check your levels of tension and your posture, relaxing muscles and allowing your head to float back up if necessary.
4. **Find a friendly face**. In your presentation, find one or two people who are more engaged with you and looking happier. Spend more time speaking directly to them and worry less about those looking blank or severe. Sometimes the most miserable-looking audience members are actually really enjoying themselves!

Follow-up

5. **Don't obsess**. Successful speakers always consider both positives and negatives from a presentation and then give themselves a break. Unsuccessful speakers focus on the things they think didn't go well, the people they spotted who looked less happy – they allow themselves to fall into a self-defeating cycle of self-criticism.

School example

Apple Grove Primary School has planned a whole-staff training session on a new behaviour policy. Sarah, an Assistant Headteacher needs to design and deliver a presentation. She is supported by a behaviour consultant.

She begins with some informal conversations with a variety of staff to find out what they already know on the topic. Sarah checks understanding of key vocabulary and concepts and looks for any terms or ideas that everyone already knows which can save time.

Sarah has been tasked with communicating the new behaviour policy, but she quickly realises that simply copying and pasting it on to slides and reading it out will be counter-productive and a waste of time. Instead, she decides to illustrate key elements with concrete examples.

As much of the behaviour policy is about routines and responses, Sarah decides to use some strategic, short video clips. She keeps the clips very short and decides to play them through twice. On the second play, she plans to pause at set points and uses a simple red circle to highlight one or two elements that are taking place along with a label or a few words.

Initially she plans to print out handouts for every member of staff. After some reflection, she decides that the handouts will be more of a distraction during the learning process as some participants' attention will be drawn to future slides when she is currently trying to engage them with an idea on the current one. Instead, she prepares handouts to distribute afterwards with an edited subset of key ideas.

After an initial run-through with one teacher and one teaching assistant, she realises that the activities that she has designed during the session need support in the presentation. In one, she had a very full slide with a question for discussion plus a summary of some key ideas. She improves the process by simplifying the slide to have only the main question plus 3 simple bullet points to describe what participants need to do. She creates a handout with the summary of key ideas. Participants are now clear that the slide is where to look for the question and for instructions about the task. When they are clear on that, they can focus on the handout for the key bullet points.

Checklists

For presenters

- ☐ Each slide presents one main idea, I have simplified as much as I can.
- ☐ There are no distracting visual elements left for me to remove on each slide.
- ☐ Each slide uses only two or three text styles and fonts are simple and readable.
- ☐ Key ideas are presented with complementary visuals, short labels and narration.
- ☐ I have used a number of short, concrete examples to turn abstract ideas into familiar ones.
- ☐ I have familiarised myself with the required narration as well as the order of slides so that I can concentrate on effective delivery, questioning and feedback.

Considerations for key audiences

For presenters

- Increase the amount of time you give yourself for slide design.
- Plan for at least two 'dry runs' of any important presentation.
- Be alert for visual and auditory distractions.
- Less is more.

For school leaders

- Invest time in effective presentation materials and set a high bar of expected quality. Your staff will thank you for it.
- Set aside time for creating, editing and refining presentation materials.
- Plan time for presenters to practise and memorise key content.

For governors

- Check the minimum expectations of presentations to staff.
- Ask staff to give you feedback on the quality of presentations and delivery that they regularly experience.

For system leaders

- Invest in high-quality presentation materials as well as time for presenters to familiarise and customise them.
- Apply the science of teacher learning and demand the highest possible standards of presentation and delivery.
- Ensure that presentations are accessible to all audiences and that they respect the time and professionalism of the audiences.

Further reading

Cordingley, P., Higgins, S., Greany, T., Buckler, N., Coles-Jordan, D., Crisp, B., Saunders, L., & Coe, R. (2015). *Developing Great Teaching* – A review of what works in professional development. http://TDTrust.org/about/dgt

School Governing Boards and CPD (2014). – An article by Clare Collins of the National Governors' Association for the Teacher Development Trust. http://tdtrust.org/school-governing-boards-and-cpd-2

Deans for Impact (2016). *Practice with Purpose: The Emerging Science of Teacher Expertise.* Austin, TX: Deans for Impact. https://deansforimpact.org/wp-content/uploads/2016/12/Practice-with-Purpose_FOR-PRINT_113016.pdf

Burn, K. Hagger, H., & Mutton, T. (2015). *Beginning Teachers' Learning: Making Experience Count.* Northwich, UK: Critical Publishing.

Note

1 Kennedy, M. (2006). Knowledge and Vision in Teaching. *Journal of Teacher Education*, 57 (3): 205–11 – quoted in Burn, K., Hagger, H., & Mutton, T. *Beginning Teachers' Learning: Making Experience Count* (Critical Guides for Teacher Educators) (Kindle Locations 1677–1678). Northwich, UK: Critical Publishing. Kindle Edition.

Epilogue

In common with many countries around the world, England is currently facing a huge challenge in recruiting and retaining both teachers and leaders. Whilst the press is rarely full of good news, the media appears to be endlessly full of burnt-out teachers.

We know from every school that we visit that our schools are filled with dedicated, hard-working staff who are desperate to achieve improvements for their children. Yet, we also know that in only some of these schools are these staff empowered to achieve this.

That reads as a depressing end to a book. But it isn't depressing, it should fill us with hope.

We have an answer that can help our children succeed and our teachers thrive. If we can get the support and development right, if we can redirect the focus on the organisational edge, if we can enable the collective wisdom of the profession to reach every teacher and every school, then we can support and empower the best possible education system.

This book is a manifesto for how schools can reach this vision in practice. Our belief is that with some key steps in place, we can see the changes we all aspire to see. We really hope this book helps you reach that.

What next for the profession?

We are encouraged to see some significant changes for teachers in England. In the last five years, the language around professional development has changed. We are seeing many more grassroots movements for sharing and learning (WomenEd, Northern Rocks), we are seeing a profession that is demanding a strong evidence base and wants to use it (ResearchEd, the Education Endowment Foundation), and we are seeing the beginnings of a new way for our profession to collaborate, learn, mobilise and advocate through the Chartered College of Teaching. These are all exciting initiatives that are working to build a stronger and more successful system.

Yet, this is urgent. Teachers and students are being failed by competing pressures and lack of resources. We still need to see significant sector change:

- Professional development should be something that all staff in school are entitled to. Professional development time should be protected in every school.
- We should invest in the development of leaders and teachers who can best meet student needs. This is the most effective and sustainable investment we should make. Schools need funding so that they can protect and invest in staff professional learning.

■ We need to harness and share the collective wisdom in the profession. There needs to be a national system through which teachers and staff can recognise high-quality expertise to support and enhance their professional learning.

Finally, we have a call for you, the reader. We have to change how we talk about professional learning. Go out and chat to your colleagues. Celebrate what you're doing. Talk about what you're doing. Let's put learning back at the centre of what we all do.

Index

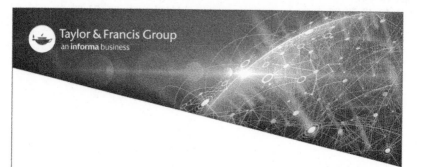